After Life
of the
Soul–Mender

ℬ   ℛ

The Later Family

of

Henry Hercock
(1811–1881)

(Part Two of the Accounts of the Lives of his Immediate Family)

– by Alan B. W. Flowerday –

After Life of the Soul–Mender

The Later Family

of

Henry Hercock
(1811–1881)

(Part Two of the Accounts of the Lives of his Immediate Family)

Published 15th August 2011,
to mark the 200th Anniversary of Henry Hercock's birth

Copyright © 2011, Alan B. W. Flowerday

All rights reserved to the Author

Published by Alan B. W. Flowerday,
"The Quails", School Road, Thurgarton, Norwich, Norfolk, NR11 7PG, England

Cover design by Claire Knight

Printed by Barnwell Print Limited,
Dunkirk, Aylsham, Norfolk NR11 6SU, England

ISBN: 978-0-9569262-1-0

Remembering with Honour:–
Henry Hercock (1811–1881)
Susannah Hercock, née Hayes (1813–1907)

✝

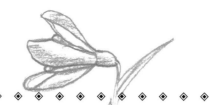

◈ ◈ ◈ ◈ ◈ ◈ ◈ ◈ ◈ ◈ ◈ ◈ ◈ ◈ ◈ ◈ ◈ ◈ ◈

For my Father
Laurence William Flowerday (1910 – 1999)
who gave me an enduring interest in family history,
and our 'HERCOCK' ancestors in particular,
from my very early days of boyhood
From nature.

– He is now sorely missed –

He was the second child and only son of parents
Richard Robert William Flowerday (1883 – 1923)
and
Ruth Flowerday, née Hercock (1882 – 1938)

◈ ◈ ◈ ◈ ◈ ◈ ◈ ◈ ◈ ◈ ◈ ◈ ◈ ◈ ◈ ◈ ◈ ◈ ◈

flower in Pendant

SNOWDROP.

The background illustration on this page
is taken from the school drawing book of
Laurence William Flowerday,
and dates from the early 1920s

After Life of the Soul–Mender

CONTENTS

❖ ❖ ❖ ❖ ❖ ❖ ❖ ❖ ❖ ❖ ❖ ❖ ❖ ❖ ❖ ❖ ❖

After Life of the Soul–Mender

The Later Family

of

Henry Hercock

(1811–1881)

(Part Two of the Accounts of the Lives of his Immediate Family)

❊ ❊❊ ❊❊ ❊❊ ❊❊ ❊❊ ❊❊ ❊

a 'HERCOCK' family study

❊ ❊❊ ❊❊ ❊❊ ❊❊ ❊❊ ❊❊ ❊

∞ *Alan B. W. Flowerday* ∞

INTRODUCTION

Status of this work vis–à–vis previous works

My earlier works **Making News in Potton** (2002) and **Orphans of a Grievous Fate** (2008) detail the life and work of the entrepreneurially talented William Henry Hercock (the latter work further relates what became of his children who were orphaned when still very young); whilst **The Life and Times of Charles James Hercock (1848–1929) : Man of Purpose** (2008) is the principal source of information on the life and work of this multi–faceted businessman – younger brother of William Henry – who found success in local trade (a particular aspect of his printing work is also included in **Making News in Potton**).

Extensive further research conducted since those three works were published has led to the need to revise information and views concerning certain aspects of the lives of the people involved, so that, wherever possible and appropriate, the most up–to–date detail about them appears in this work (and its immediate companion work, **The Shoe–Maker turned Soul–Mender**, to which this work is a sequel) which, thus, supersede previous works in those respects which mutually conflict or in which the previous works are seen to be deficient. Research findings (related to any and all of the folk with whom this work is concerned) up to and including 14th May 2011 are included in this work.

❖ ❖ ❖ ❖ ❖ ❖ ❖ ❖ ❖ ❖ ❖ ❖

Church vs. *Chapel*

In this work the term 'Church' (or 'church') is reserved (with the sole exception stated hereinbelow) for a building or community associated with the Established religious institution of England, or Anglicanism (as it became after the Reformation). The term 'Chapel' (or 'chapel') is used for a building or community associated with any Nonconformist religion or denomination, *except* that where any such specific Nonconformist institution uses the term 'Church' in naming any of its records or archives to which reference is made herein then that naming, including the term 'Church', is faithfully used herein.

❖ ❖ ❖ ❖ ❖ ❖ ❖ ❖ ❖ ❖ ❖ ❖

Special Thanks ...

... to Philip Neville, a friend and researcher into the history of Baptist Chapels, who has unstintingly given of his time and energies to help me with much detailed research, contributing a large number of documents which he sourced for me, and who has provided much other information and assistance some of which opened up aspects of Henry Hercock's life previously unknown to me.

Acknowledgements

Many people have contributed to this work in different ways over the years I have been gathering information towards it. Whilst I am grateful to them all, it is not feasible to name them all personally here. All those whom it is reasonable to name – on the strength of their contributions to this work – are listed below (in alphabetical order of surname). The names of a few professional researchers who have been responsible for making spectacular finds of quite astonishing information to go into this book are specifically included. I wish, also, to thank my wife, Ann, for all her patience and quiet acceptance that I was otherwise engaged during all the long hours of both research and writing, whether out and about or in my study; this has enabled me to work towards completing this story with the least possible fuss.

Principal Personal Acknowledgements

(The following people live (or lived) in England unless otherwise stated)

Mrs. Irene R. Baker, née Flowerday (late sister of the Author's father) – great–granddaughter
of Henry & Susannah Hercock

Mrs. Beryl E. Croft (Tasmania) – great–granddaughter of Henry & Susannah Hercock

Mr. Stan K. Evers (Potton) – Pastor of Potton Baptist Church
(formerly the Strict Baptist Chapel where Henry Hercock was Pastor, 1866–1879)

Mr. Laurence W. Flowerday (late father of the Author) – great–grandson
of Henry & Susannah Hercock

Mr. Robert Hercock (Bristol) – unrelated to the 'HERCOCK' line of this account

Miss Marion G. Hyde (Hove) – Librarian of The Gospel Standard Baptist Library

Mr. John R. Jarman (Barton–on–Sea) – great–great–grandson of Henry & Susannah Hercock

Mrs. Mollie B. Lucy (Romford) – great–great–granddaughter of Henry & Susannah Hercock

Mr. Philip J. Neville (Tunbridge Wells) – friend, with interests in, *inter alia,* the history
of Baptists and their Chapels

Mr. Robert Parish (Needingworth) – step–grandson
of Mary Ann Sawyer ('Polly') Senescall, née Hercock

Ms. Rosie Taylor (London) – professional genealogical researcher (deceased November 2010)

Mr. David J. Woodruff (Dunstable) – Librarian of The Strict Baptist Historical Society

Mrs. Patricia R. Yates (Potton & Bedford) – Founder Member of Potton History Society Archives

List of Illustrations, with Credits

The following is a complete list of illustrations included in this work.
See the Notes at the end of the following Table.

Caption to Illustration	Page	Additional Description and/or Credit	Credit, inc. Copyright © owner and any Reference
The gravitas of Henry Hercock is palpable in this engraving from his **Memoir**	14	from the book's flyleaf	'HERCOCK' Family Archive
Advertisement from The Gospel Standard of June 1882	15	courtesy of Miss Marion G. Hyde (Librarian)	The Gospel Standard Baptist Library
Grave memorial at Braunston–in–Rutland of Henry Hercock's sister, Mary Springthorpe, and her husband	C1		© Alan B. W. Flowerday 2009
The handwriting of Henry Hercock's fifth daughter, Susanna	16	a true serendipitous find	Alan B. W. Flowerday Family History Archive
Ruth Hercock as a toddler	23	circa 1885	'HERCOCK' Family Archive
Orphanage Discharge Register Entry for Polly	24	reproduced with permission, and courtesy of Mr. J. Marsh (latterly Chief Executive)	The George Müller Foundation
Grave memorial of John Sturton, Broadway Cemetery, Peterborough	27		© Alan B. W. Flowerday 2009
Queen Victoria's Golden Jubilee Concert programme printed by Charles James Hercock	C2	reproduced with permission, and courtesy of the Society's Committee	Potton History Society Archives
William and Mary Hayes Baxter at Hitchin	28	reproduced with permission, and courtesy of R. W. Hurlock and Mrs. D. Simmons	R. W. Hurlock
Grave memorial of Henry Hercock's elder brother, William	30		© Alan B. W. Flowerday 2009
The entire Duddington family, circa 1895	34	reproduced with permission	Brenda Duddington
A bill issued by Charles James Hercock in 1895	C3	reproduced with permission, and courtesy of Mr. N. Lutt (Archivist)	Bedfordshire & Luton Archives Service (Ref. Z723/100/53)
Victor Rex (left) and John Frederick Hurlock, circa 1900	36	reproduced with permission, and courtesy of Mrs. S. Haugli	Descendants of John Hurlock
Detail from a bill issued in 1893 by Charles James Hercock	37	reproduced with permission, and courtesy of the Society's Committee	Potton History Society Archives

[continued →

Caption to Illustration	Page	Additional Description and/or Credit	Credit, inc. Copyright © owner and any Reference
Potton Baptist Chapel Church Book extract, 1894	39	reproduced with permission, and courtesy of Pastor Stan K. Evers	Potton Baptist Church
Fob watch in a satin–lined case inscribed with Willy Hercock's name and other details	C4	reproduced with permission	© Mrs. Mollie B. Lucy 2011
Willy Hercock was widely respected	41	reproduced with permission	Mrs. Mollie B. Lucy
Joseph Oldfield	44		–
Godmanchester Particular Baptist Chapel	47	courtesy of Miss Marion G. Hyde (Librarian)	The Gospel Standard Baptist Library
Ernie Hercock as a young man	53		'HERCOCK' Family Archive
Susannah Hercock in a 4-generations photograph, 1902	C5	reproduced with permission	John R. Jarman
Nellie Emily Hurlock and her children, circa 1909	62	reproduced with permission, and courtesy of Mr. & Mrs. F. Hurlock, and Mr. & Mrs. D. Haugli	Descendants of John Hurlock
Dora May Hurlock on her wedding day, 1928	63	reproduced with permission, and courtesy of Mrs. M. Hurlock	Descendants of John Hurlock
Potton Market Square in the early twentieth century	64	from a surviving postcard posted in 1905	Alan B. W. Flowerday Family History Archive
Walter, Edie and their children at Romford	66	reproduced with permission	Mrs. Mollie B. Lucy
Susannah Hercock's grave memorial at Godmanchester	C1		© Alan B. W. Flowerday 2009
The artistry of Susannah Hercock's grave memorial	69		© Alan B. W. Flowerday 2002
Anna Julia Hercock's grave memorial at Godmanchester	C6		© Alan B. W. Flowerday 2009
Charles James Hercock and his wife Mary Anne, née Baxter	73	Dunstable, circa 1910	'HERCOCK' Family Archive
Wedding photograph of Richard Robert William Flowerday and Ruth Hercock, 1908	C7	Dunstable	'HERCOCK' Family Archive
Edith Hercock as a young woman	74	circa 1908	'HERCOCK' Family Archive
Great Aunt Mary and Polly on Ruth Hercock's wedding day	74	Dunstable, 1908	'HERCOCK' Family Archive

[continued →

Caption to Illustration	Page	Additional Description and/or Credit	Credit, inc. Copyright © owner and any Reference
Grave memorial of Polly's husband, George Ambrose	76	at Godmanchester	© Alan B. W. Flowerday 2009
Laurie and Rene Flowerday	77		Alan B. W. Flowerday Family History Archive
Part of Godmanchester – showing the location of the Hercocks' home in 1910	78	reproduced with permission, and courtesy of Mr. P. Saunders	Cambridgeshire Archives & Local Studies (Huntingdonshire Archives: Land Values Duties Map, 1910)
Sisters Susanna Markwell and Mary Hayes Baxter, circa 1909	80		'HERCOCK' Family Archive
Polly Senescall in later life, with two of her step–grandchildren	85	reproduced with permission	Robert Parish
The house in Post Street formerly occupied by the Hercocks	86	identified from the 1910 Land Values Duties records	© Alan B. W. Flowerday 2010
Brothers Bertram, Albert and Wilfred Henry Hercock as young men	87	montage; individual images taken from a larger group photograph, 1921	© Alan B. W. Flowerday 2008
Eliza Jane Hercock's grave memorial at Godmanchester	C6		© Alan B. W. Flowerday 2009
Victor Rex Hurlock	97	reproduced with permission, and courtesy of Mr. & Mrs. F. Hurlock, and Mr. & Mrs. D. Haugli	Descendants of John Hurlock
Eddie Bowen with his wife and infant daughter	98		'HERCOCK' Family Archive
Mary Hayes and William Baxter's grave memorial at Godmanchester	99		© Alan B. W. Flowerday 2009
Memorial Plaque: Eddie Bowen	C8	reproduced with permission, and courtesy of Mr. & Mrs. M. B. Large and Mrs. O. C. Moore	© Malcolm B. Large 2008
Grave memorial of Helen Letitia and Joseph Duddington	101		© Alan B. W. Flowerday 2002
Charles James Hercock	103		'HERCOCK' Family Archive
A surviving relic of the former Particular Baptist Chapel, Godmanchester	C8	found in a private house garden in Godmanchester; photograph used with permission of the house owner	© Alan B. W. Flowerday 2010

[continued →

Caption to Illustration	Page	Additional Description and/or Credit	Credit, inc. Copyright © owner and any Reference
Clifford Hurlock in his prime	114	reproduced with permission, and courtesy of Barbara J. Hurlock and Susan C. Warwick	Barbara J. Hurlock and Susan C. Warwick
Henry Ernest Hurlock as a young man	120	reproduced with permission, and courtesy of Mrs. M. Hurlock	Descendants of John Hurlock
Master Mariner: the late Peter Hurlock	120	reproduced with permission, and courtesy of Mrs. M. Hurlock	© Mrs. M. Hurlock
What's in an address ...	121	from a surviving postcard posted in 1905	Alan B. W. Flowerday Family History Archive
... and what's in a message!	121	from a surviving postcard posted in 1905	Alan B. W. Flowerday Family History Archive

NOTES

All included illustrations obtained from identified sources are reproduced with permission; the Author acknowledges with gratitude permissions of the owners and/or suppliers of all illustrations for their use in this work. Ownership of Copyright in any illustration is indicated by © in Column 4 above, where it has been possible to identify the current owner.

Cover illustrations:–

Background:

Part of the Headstone of Susannah Hercock
['HERCOCK' Family Archive]

Foreground (top left to bottom right):

Susannah Hercock, née Hayes;
Mary Hayes Baxter, née Hercock;
Helen Letitia Duddington, née Hercock;
Susanna Markwell, née Hercock;
Charles James Hercock
['HERCOCK' Family Archive]

After Life of the Soul–Mender

PART ONE

A Very Particular Family : Henry Hercock's Widow and Progeny

PROLOGUE

After Shock

FIREBRAND PARTICULAR BAPTIST MINISTER Henry Hercock had just died. It was late August 1881. Stunned by his departure into the after life, his deeply grieving family must have questioned their whole reason for existence, enquiring of their God how it could be that the guiding light of their lives had been subjected to such physical and emotional torment as the highly aggressive cancer which had claimed his life had slowly, agonisingly, encroached on his whole being until he could take no more.

Just a couple of weeks earlier Henry had reached his seventieth birthday; of course, it had not been an occasion for celebration, for it was abundantly clear that this was to be his last and, in any case, the tumours were already so far advanced that no–one in his close family could countenance any form of merriment. Instead, this 'three score years and ten' milestone in his life had probably been more about reflection on Henry's past life and accomplishments, and a fearsome wondering about the future.

Henry had come to be a Minister rather late in life: indeed, he'd been about forty years old by the time he assumed the formal mantle of 'minister'. As a teenager he'd been an improbable candidate for such an elevated spiritual situation, for he'd run badly off the rails whilst undergoing an apprenticeship to become a Shoe–Maker. However, coming from a family background of common decency and traditional middle class farming self–discipline, Henry's father had observed with utter horror what was becoming of his boy in the seamy leather–cutting room, and had paid the necessary compensation to have the lad released early from what would otherwise have been seven long years in this devil's cauldron – with heaven knows what outcome for Henry and his future. As it was, Henry – after just three years in such squalid surroundings and among other teenage apprentices whose somewhat debauched conduct had lured him into their ways of living – had fallen easy prey to the call of Satan, quickly sloughing off the sheath of moral rectitude that was his childhood protection to become nothing more than another wayward youth. Thus, by the time Henry was returned to the sobering environment of his family home in Wing, Rutland, he was changed radically from the clean–living young man who had said fond goodbyes to his parents just a few years before.

But Henry was fortunate in having a guardian angel who now stepped in to take the late teenager in hand: for Henry had descended to such depths of moral turpitude that even he was appalled by his own conduct, and, in an effort to reform his being, turned to religion. He now attended Church – no doubt this would have been the Parish Church of Wing, as his was a stalwart Church of England family –

and took to reading religious works, including the Bible. This was the tentative beginning of a painfully protracted process of conversion. Progressing through various stages – none without profound mental anguish – the young adult toyed with the General Baptists after having left the Anglicans behind for their uninspiring (to him) ways; but before long he'd had revealed to him what he saw as flaws in the General Baptist approach to life, so he quit them, too, to throw his lot in with a group of Particular Baptists. This happened after he'd been taken by the apparently more truthful and honest preaching of one John Carter from Peterborough whom Henry heard with deepening interest. Moving to Oakham, here Henry aligned himself more closely with this emerging new group, and fell under the influence of the great William Tiptaft – one of the mid–19th Century's most notable propounders of the errors of Anglicanism and promoters of the non–ritualistic Particular Baptist movement.

At Oakham, Henry – who'd been baptised into his new faith not many years before – not only worked as a Shoe–Maker with his own workshop, but also found further guidance under another of the era's foremost Particular Baptist names in the person of Joseph Charles Philpot. So it was that Henry Hercock eventually joined with others to form the Oakham Strict Baptist Chapel that was known as 'Providence'. He became a Deacon here in the mid–1840s. But he was cut out to become much more: highly intelligent, and with a special brand of speaking which brought him to the attention of folk who were crying out

for more of the true Word of God, he was unwittingly thrust forward – first into the garb of Lay Preacher, but soon into the cloak and whole being of a fully–fledged Minister.

It was now about 1850, and Henry became attached to an incipient Calvinist Baptist group at the small village of Whissendine (to the north–west from Oakham). The next step, taken within a very few months, was to see him elevated to the post of first Minister of the newly–formed Zion Chapel in Whissendine.

From this point he'd gone on to become Pastor of the North Street Baptist Chapel in Peterborough (here he was almost back on home soil as he'd been born in the village of Laxton, Northamptonshire), later moving to the market town of Potton, Bedfordshire, where he held the Pastorate of the Strict Baptist Chapel for thirteen years before, finally, moving to Leeds in 1879. It was here that he died, though not before having trod upon the next step up the ladder of the Strict Baptist movement – when he associated himself, in the early 1870s, with The Gospel Standard Aid Society, a national body in whose inauguration he was involved and on to whose management Committee he was subsequently elected.

Thus, at the time of his demise, not only had he established himself as a considerable presence in the national governance – tenuously undeveloped as it then was – of the Strict Baptist movement; but also he had, through years of down–to–business, no–nonsense preaching in dozens of deprived, rural communities, and larger towns and cities where spiritual aridity had given him a ready audience, become a considerable force to be reckoned with, earning himself a reputation for plain, passionate speaking – taking an outspoken stand against other, ritualistic religions and non–believers, promoting instead his own faith which offered poor souls salvation and an after life of everlasting peace. From about 1861 Henry Hercock had devoted his energies entirely to this cause, leaving behind for good his leather–working tools and using instead the tools which God had endowed in his person, to work on the minds of folk who were ripe for receiving spiritual meaning into their humdrum lives.

Against this backdrop, Hercock's death opened up a void of immense proportions, both for his large flock of hearers and supporters, spread across a wide swathe of England (especially Eastern England and the Midlands which had been the main arena of his extensive visiting preaching), and for his family. None could have felt the pain of his passing more acutely than his devoted widow, Susannah; though the couple's nine adult offspring – to most of whom Henry had been a shining beacon of a father and moral leader – also must have deeply grieved his departure. There were also many grandchildren, to some of whom Henry had been far more than just a grandfather.

Turning away from the site of Henry's grave in Leeds' Woodhouse Cemetery, his family and many friends, colleagues and supporters returned to their homes nurturing an unfathomable sense of loss. More than this, however, his family was faced with pressing practical problems which required early resolution. Their time for grieving, was, then, overlaid with a kind of driving force of everyday life which had to take urgent priority. Putting much of their raw emotion aside for the time being, they turned their unenthusiastic minds to the business at hand – and set about determining the course for the future.

❖ ❖ ❖ ❖ ❖ ❖ ❖ ❖ ❖ ❖ ❖ ❖ ❖ ❖ ❖ ❖

A note about the Memoir of Henry Hercock

Shortly after Henry Hercock's death his family arranged for the publication of his **Memoir**; compiled from notes which Henry himself had written, and complemented with some of his surviving letters and other material, the small book was publicly available from early summer 1882. For convenience, the work may be considered to consist of three separate parts. These are: (1) a part based on notes which Henry Hercock himself had written – this comprises Pages 9 to 47 of the published work; (2) a part based on Henry's daughter Mary Hayes Baxter's recollections of her father and his work, supplemented by memories of other family members – this comprises Pages 47 to 56 of the published work; and (3) a part comprised of assorted letters and other writings penned by both Henry and other folk – this comprises Pages 57 to 120 of the published work.

I make reference, in this book, to some of the content of the third part, only, of Henry's **Memoir** and these references are accompanied by the code 'OTR' to indicate their source. A full, detailed analysis of the **Memoir** is undertaken in my other book, **The Shoe–Maker turned Soul–Mender**, which is the forerunner of this book; the *Memoir* forms a framework of that work.

❖ ❖ ❖ ❖ ❖ ❖ ❖ ❖ ❖ ❖ ❖ ❖ ❖ ❖ ❖ ❖ ❖ ❖

THE FRUITS OF HIS LABOURS

Family Adjustments

First and foremost Henry Hercock's family needed to consider with some urgency the position of his widow, Susannah, for her age alone predicated against her remaining up north, in Leeds, now that the leading light of her life was no longer there to help and provide for her. Also, her young grandson, the orphaned Walter Charles James Hercock – then about 11½ years old – had been living with his grandparents and still had some years ahead when his educational and other needs required something more than Susannah alone could manage.

Ironically, Henry and Susannah had been intending to leave Leeds [***Memoir***, Pages 104 & 105 (OTR) – letter to Mr. Hind, dated 7ᵗʰ April 1881], and at the time of Henry's death had already given notice of their intention to move out of their house at the end of the year [***Memoir***, Pages 109 & 110 (OTR) – letter to Miss Howitt, dated 30ᵗʰ June 1881]. Quite where they thought they might next go was undecided, as Henry had been awaiting the opening of a suitable *'door'* and of a *'making the way plain'*, but it seems more than likely that they hoped to return south to familiar surroundings in which they'd shared most of their lives together.

However, Henry's death put an entirely different complexion on the matter of when and where Susannah and Walter might go. Without wishing to engage the topic with what might have been seen as undue haste, nevertheless Charles James Hercock (Henry and Susannah's eldest surviving son, otherwise known affectionately as 'CJ') will have taken it upon himself, perhaps, to open discussions whilst he and his wife, Mary Anne, were still in Leeds following Henry's funeral. They could not dally here, as their busy, town centre shop in Potton required their presence, so important family matters such as this – to which 'CJ's input was likely to be significant – needed to be dealt with promptly. Thus, it was a time when all concerned needed to draw deeply on their inner reserves and their faith, to help them grapple with such important matters as future living arrangements.

Meanwhile, whilst such adjustments were under discussion, in the melting pot and being put into effect, news of Henry's death was spreading. Back at home in Potton, 'CJ' and Mary Anne, and others, will already have alerted Friends at the Baptist Chapel, as well as others in the town and environs, of Henry's passing, and the following note was entered in **The Church Book of Potton Baptist Chapel**:–

> Mᵣ Hercock late Pastor of this Church, died at Leeds on Lords day morning, August 28ᵗʰ 1881. aged 70 years – see "Gospel Standard" 477 page [sic] – Octᵣ 1881 – He was buried in the Leeds Cemetry [sic] by Mᵣ Coughtrey of Nottingham. Six God–fearing man [sic] carried him to the grave, and some of

the congregation from the room in Basinghall S*t*, where he preached his last sermon, sang that beautiful hymn of Berridge's over his grave, beginning:

"O happy soul, who safely passed,
Thy weary warfare here;
Arrived at Jesu's seat at last
And ended all thy care." —

> Verbatim quotations herein from **The Church Book of Potton Baptist Chapel** are by permission of Pastor Stan K. Evers of Potton Baptist Church.

And, spreading the news more widely, **The Christian's Monthly Record** printed a brief announcement of the death: '*On Aug. 28th, aged 70, Mr. Hercock, minister of the gospel, of Leeds, late of Potton.*' [**The Christian's Monthly Record**, October 1881: page 284]

Furthermore, 'CJ' busied himself to ease his pain: he began to confront his grief head–on by starting to pen an Obituary of his father – which was soon published in **The Gospel Standard**. (This Obituary is reproduced in full in my companion book, **The Shoe–Maker turned Soul–Mender**.)

Messages of condolence and support poured in from far and wide in the early days following Henry's passing. These will have been of some comfort to the family in their most intensive period of grieving. Following on from the publication of Reverend Hercock's Obituary in **The Gospel Standard**, his old friend, Mr. W. Sharpe of Ramsgate, with whom Henry's association went back to their time together at Oakham, sent to the Editor of **The Gospel Standard** a poignant tribute to Hercock which was later to be included in Henry's *Memoir*. [*Memoir*, Pages 57–60 (OTR)] In it, Sharpe recalls how they heard the preaching of Mr. Philpot at Oakham; and, earlier, William Tiptaft, recounting the tumultuous scenes in those far off, heady days as ordinary folk poured in from villages near and far to hear this great man; and relates how he and Henry had actually met long before the Baptist Chapel at Oakham had had its formal beginning. '*Our old friend, Mr. H*[ercock]*, was a regular hearer at Oakham, and was much attached to the place, the people, and the minister, from whom he had received much profit,*' says Mr. Sharpe. Some years later, after Henry had begun his own preaching, '*... many a weary journey has he taken, walking to and fro to serve for scant reward the poor people assembled together ...*' continues Sharpe's testimony. And, speaking about his friend's regular visits to preach at Swinstead and environs, Mr. Sharpe says '*... he was highly esteemed,*' [*Memoir*, Pages 59 & 60 (OTR)] thus echoing the fact that Henry had been spoken of by Swinstead folk as '*our dear Mr. Hercock*' [From the Obituary of Mr. Thomas Camm of Swinstead, published in **The Gospel Standard**, March 1872: pages 186 and 187].

Just how extensively Henry Hercock is likely to have been missed by his regular hearers and the Strict Baptist community at large is difficult to judge as we have no comprehensive, central record of the Baptist Chapels with which he had had some kind of association down the years. But cogent evidence of places at which he is known to have preached makes plain that his reputation and popularity in Baptist circles greatly exceeded even what are hinted at by the many places he names in his *Memoir* and through his personal letters reproduced therein – the strength of his connections with Bedfordshire and Lincolnshire are especially evident, but the overarching geographical spread is quite remarkable.

❖ ❖ ❖ ❖ ❖ ❖ ❖ ❖ ❖ ❖ ❖ ❖ ❖ ❖ ❖ ❖ ❖ ❖ ❖

Family Affairs in the 1880s

Memoir of The Man

Now, although Henry's death created an awful chasm not only in his family, but also among his many friends, Baptist followers, and – not least – ministerial colleagues up and down the country, there was no immediate recognition amongst his family that written memoirs of Henry's life could be of general interest. However, it soon became apparent that there was a demand for such a work, for from several of his colleagues and supporters came requests and encouragement for the publication of Henry's memoirs. As his daughter, Mary, knew of her father's compilations of assorted writings and notes which he had been intending to publish, she soon began actively to consider the possibility of sorting these, adding the content of various letters her father had written – particularly during his final days – and completing the whole with the addition of her own and other family members' recollections of Henry and his life.

Gradually the idea of a small book of her father's published memoirs took shape. Mary was heartened by the persuasiveness of some Baptist Friends who convinced her of the worth of disseminating an account of her father's life and work. So, with the ready help of her brother, Charles James, who not only had the requisite printing skills, but also the equipment and general setup in the print–room at his Potton premises, the go–ahead to proceed with this ambitious project was given once the celebrated Baptist publisher of the period, John Gadsby of London, had given the venture his backing.

After several months of intensive work on the part of Mary and her brother, 'CJ', their father's *Memoir* was ready; 'CJ' had printed it himself – nothing short of a labour of love; it was the most ambitious printing project he'd ever undertaken. The little book, measuring four–and–

The gravitas of Henry Hercock is palpable in this engraving from his *Memoir*

three–quarter inches wide, seven–and–one–eighth inches high, and barely three–eighths of an inch thick after binding (in its standard hardcover version), is what emerged from the printing press at Potton and, having been published at London, to sell at various prices depending on the chosen style of binding and finish, is testament to, firstly, Henry Hercock the man and his sincerely–held convictions which drove him onwards through his adult life, and, secondly, his elder surviving son, Charles James Hercock, the man who sweated in his small, grimy print–room to bring his father's being and work back to life in this new sense. The sense that the **Memoir** is *the* most tangible, undying legacy of the remarkable man who was Henry Hercock.

The introduction to the book was penned by Mary Hayes Baxter, whilst her father's old friend, Mr. W. Sharpe, wrote the book's Preface which he dated 31st March 1882. When the **Memoir** first went on sale (on 15th May 1882) and was promoted through Christian journals and bookshops, it's unlikely it created a vast amount of interest. Too specialised, and of appeal to a relatively narrow audience among the general public, nevertheless it will have been welcomed by his most dedicated followers and supporters – so it would have been in Baptist communities in which Henry had been a familiar face, as well as in wider family circles, that it will have found its greatest interest and champions.

John Gadsby – who had rubbed shoulders with Hercock many times at

---

Now ready, price, half roan, marble edges, and photographic portrait, 2s. 6d.; limp cloth, with portrait from woodcut, 1s. 6d.; paper covers, 1s.,
Memoir of Henry Hercock, late Minister of the Gospel, Leeds, &c., containing Call by Grace, Call to the Ministry, Ministerial Labours, and Death; with numerous Extracts from Letters, and a Sermon, and Preface by Mr. SHARP, of Ramsgate. Photographs, with autograph, 6d. each.

London: J. Gadsby, 18, Bouverie Street, Fleet Street, London, E.C. To be had of Mrs. Hercock, 117, New Norton Street, New Radford, Nottingham; any Bookseller; and of C. J. Hercock, Potton, Beds, who will forward same per post on receipt of 13, 20, or 33 stamps.

Friends of the late Mr. Hercock are requested to circulate this little work as widely as possible, in a spiritual point of view, for the honour of God and the comfort of the living family, and providentially for the benefit of the widow.

Advertisement from The Gospel Standard of June 1882

---

meetings in London and was, therefore, well known to the family – had agreed to donate all profits from the sale of Henry's **Memoir** to his widow (an indication that his death had left her in fairly straitened circumstances), so Baptist friends were given every encouragement to purchase their own copies as well as to take additional copies for onward sale.

Whatever their individual circumstances, it is probable that most, if not all, of Henry and Susannah's progeny bought their own copies of Henry's **Memoir**. Living at Biggleswade, Bedfordshire, Susanna Allen (Henry's fifth–born daughter) and her husband, Thomas, certainly purchased a copy of Henry's **Memoir** which Susanna herself must have cherished over many, many years ahead.

Thomas and Susanna Allen's copy of Henry's *Memoir* survives to this day: by a remarkable turn of events, it came into my ownership during April 2011 after it had originally been lent to me by The Gospel Standard Baptist Library. Written in Susanna's hand, an unprinted page preceding the flyleaf has a written inscription stating the date, 28th May 1882, on which the book was obtained. Many years later the names of the original owners were amended to reflect Susanna's change of marital surname and status.

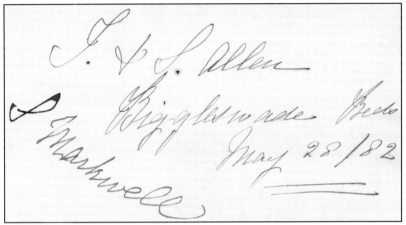

The handwriting of Henry Hercock's fifth daughter, Susanna

◉ ◉ ◉ ◉ ◉ ◉ ◉ ◉ ◉ ◉ ◉ ◉ ◉ ◉ ◉ ◉ ◉

A New Phase of Life

The Baptist faith that Henry had given them, shared with them, and exhorted them to live by every moment of their lives, was, perhaps, the greatest asset that his family carried forward into their lives without him. It will have helped them cope with difficult times when memories of his voice, smile, countenance, mannerisms, touch, or other little things about him suddenly struck them when they were least expecting, causing them – on occasion – to dissolve into tears. Each will have carried such memories within in their own special way. But it would have been for Susannah, his widow, that coming to terms with his absences will have been the greatest upset, for it was she who had partnered him through all the times of their married life – the ups and downs – supporting him in his work and around the local communities in which he served; warming his bed, consulting with him on matters of the upbringing of their many children, feeding his bodily hunger from the meagre income which they had to stretch as far as possible ... and attending to the myriad other things of everyday life, freeing him to concentrate his mind on the demands of his occupation.

Initially, the decision had been taken that Susannah and Walter should leave Leeds to go to live with Lucy Ann and her children. Widowed many years previously, Lucy Ann Underwood was Henry and Susannah's second daughter; but she'd always been a bit of a handful and never had shared a particularly amicable relationship with her parents, especially Henry. Despite the long–

standing differences, at that time this decision on Susannah and Walter's living arrangements made good sense, logically: Walter would have the company of his young cousins – Lucy's three children, the eldest about the age of twelve and easily Walter's peer – and Lucy could keep an eye on her grieving mother who, in turn, would provide some companionship for her daughter. Thus, they ended up living in Nottingham, where initially they resided in the city at '117 New Norton Street, New Radford'.

The necessary adjustments were slowly made for their communal living, and young Walter and his grandmother, Susannah, gradually settled into their new environment. In recognition of the fact that Susannah was now far more vulnerable, as a widow of seventy–ish years without ample means for her own financial support, it appears very probable that Lucy's sister, Eliza Jane, took the opportunity to review her living arrangements around this time, for this was an era when family folk remained in close proximity, if possible, and offspring certainly stayed near elderly parents (whom they often cared for). Thus, it seems likely she also decided to make a new start in Nottingham, and came to live in the household. Eliza being the more able of these two sisters to find employment and manage their mother's affairs, she perhaps needed some little time to conclude existing living and working arrangements (in Cirencester), but in all probability moved to Nottingham some time in late

1883 or in 1884. Later, they moved to 272 Alfreton Road so it seems that by some time in 1884 this property housed the group consisting of Lucy's three children and Lucy herself, Susannah, Eliza Jane (possibly) and Walter. With so many squeezed under the one roof, the house must have felt rather crowded at times.

It was only during October 2008 that I discovered Susannah Hercock had lived in Nottingham with her daughter, Lucy Ann Underwood, in the period between the time of Henry's death in August 1881 and the 1891 Census. I'd been using the Internet to research various Trade Directories, and – on a mere whim – searched the Nottingham Street Directory of 1885 for 'Hercock'; I was surprised when the entry for Mrs. Susannah Hercock was the only one which reported. Immediately thereafter I searched for 'Underwood', and soon found Lucy Ann, whereupon I noticed that both women were living at the same street address. This discovery neatly fills a gap which was evident in the mid–1880s, for, importantly, it opened the way to postulate the simultaneous presence of Eliza Jane Hercock whose whereabouts in this period had been troubling me (Eliza Jane was the third–born, spinster daughter of Henry and Susannah). Then, in May 2009 I received copies of **The Gospel Standard** advertisements (for Henry's *Memoir*) which cite Henry Hercock's widow living in Nottingham way back in May 1882.

The form (as above) of the address for Mrs. Hercock, Henry's widow, is included in advertisements which appeared in May and June 1882 **wrappers of The Gospel Standard**, but investigations into Nottingham records dating between 1881 and 1883 suggest the correct address would have been 117 Norton Street, Radford, Nottingham. 'New Radford' was an Ecclesiastical Parish name – the Civil Parish was plain 'Radford' – and nowhere in that area is there listed a 'New' Norton Street. Even so, currently it is only for Henry's widow that we have documented evidence of residence at this Nottingham address, but, given that we know she was later definitely to be found living in Nottingham with her widowed daughter, Lucy Ann (for whom we have the suggestion that she, too, lived in the city earlier than the currently-documented address for her of 272 Alfreton Road – See below), it appears virtually certain that Susannah and Lucy Ann (and the others named in the main text hereabouts) all lived together at the Norton Street address from early 1882.

'New Norton Street, New Radford' was, apparently, under development and considerable expansion at the time as the address did not exist in any form in 1881, but clearly did by 1883; by all events, the family members' sojourn in Radford was to be short – as a person of a different name was listed at this address by late 1883.

Burgesses Registers list Alice Hill living at 117 Norton Street, Radford, as at 20th October 1883, and the property appears to have been empty by 1885. None of various other sources investigated shows any 'HERCOCK' or 'UNDERWOOD' person living at the address between 1881 and 1883.

Although there is no documented evidence that Walter Charles James Hercock lived in Nottingham at the time (the early– to mid–1880s), this is considered – on the balance of probabilities – the most feasible scenario, for here he would have had his young cousins for companionship.

There is no currently-known documentary evidence that Eliza Jane Hercock lived in Nottingham at any time before 1884, but that she did move there is considered a very likely scenario. The last mention of Eliza in the records of the Park Street Baptist Chapel, Cirencester, dates from 1882 – coincidentally, about the earliest time that her mother is known to have been first living in Nottingham; however, the list of Annual Subscribers to the funds of The Gospel Standard Aid Society for the year 1883 includes Eliza Jane, recording: 'Hercock, Miss E. J., Cirencester' (she paid ten shillings and sixpence); moreover, Eliza was not to appear elsewhere until several years later, so her presence in Nottingham in the period from about 1883/84 to the later 1880s would readily explain her absence elsewhere.

White's History, Gazetteer & Directory of Nottinghamshire, 1885 – Nottingham Alphabetical Directory, page 452: 'Hercock Mrs. Susannah, 272 Alfreton road'; and Nottingham Alphabetical Directory, page 524: 'Underwood Mrs. Lucy Ann, 272 Alfreton road'.

Even though all the family would have been fully committed to these re-arrangements of their personal lives, the fact that they were turning their backs on Henry's last resting place in Leeds must have been of considerable sadness and hurt to them. For, the distances from their chosen new home territories, or –

for those remaining on established home ground – were far too great to enable more than just the very occasional future visit to his grave. Although, in the early years following Henry's death, there may have been something of an annual pilgrimage to Woodhouse Cemetery by a central group of his surviving family members, as time wore on this is unlikely to have persisted until, eventually, visitors to the place where his mortal remains lay were sporadic or no more. Then it was likely to be their memories of the place, and the person interred there, that fed their undying yearning for the sound of Henry's voice, the shape of his face, and the softness of his touch.

One of the attractions of Nottingham to the Hercocks in these early years after Henry's death was the presence of their good friend, Mr. Alfred Coughtrey (a former close colleague of Henry), as the Pastor of the Chaucer Street Baptist Chapel; it appears very probable that it was to his (Coughtrey's) Chapel that the Nottingham family members tied themselves.

But it required far more than Mr. Coughtrey's appeal and that of the Chapel to hold the new 'HERCOCK' household together in harmony. Seemingly, though all concerned made a concerted effort to achieve a successful, happy outcome from their living together under the same roof, unfortunately it was not to be. Lucy was not the easiest of folk to get on with; the atmosphere soon became strained as adults and children alike began to wear each other down due to their incompatible lifestyles and ways of dealing with each other. The demands of caring for Susannah, and the fraught matter of managing family finances to the satisfaction of all, probably caused more heartache than any of them had foreseen possible, and, as it fell to Eliza to bring in much of the household income, she may have felt she had the right – perhaps disputed by Lucy Ann – to dictate to a large degree how the family's monies were used. She, the most highly intelligent and quick–witted of the two sisters living here, probably felt a rising sense of frustration with the way things were going, and knew that a resolution needed to be sought as breaking point loomed.

Once again family debate of the alternatives would have taken place, centring on a consideration of where else the group comprising Susannah and Eliza could sensibly move and yet not lose the benefits of being near some of their other close blood relations and a Chapel with a minister of their liking. Eventually, Biggleswade was selected. But this was seen as not entirely suitable for young Walter who would, if he were to accompany the adults there, be deprived of company of other young people in the household; in any case, it was – perhaps – felt that he would gain more from having a young married couple as his Guardians instead of his ageing grandmother and her middle–aged daughters. The suggestion was, thus, floated that Walter should return to Potton, where he'd been born at a time when his father, the ill–fated William Henry Hercock (who had died in the mid–1870s and soon was followed in death by his widow) had formerly been proprietor of the family business now owned and run by William Henry's younger brother, Charles James. The thinking was that young Walter should live with his Uncle Charles James and Aunt Mary Anne Hercock; here, once more he could live on the Market Square in the premises which was already very familiar to him. As a pupil of the local Board School, here he would be able to complete his primary education.

> There is no known documentary evidence of Walter Hercock's return to Potton from Leeds (or move to Nottingham) during the 1880s. However, it was common knowledge in some quarters of the wider family circle of the late 20th Century (as first told to me in the 1990s by my Aunt, Mrs. Irene Ruth Baker, née Flowerday) that the teenage Walter had been brought up in Potton by his uncle and aunt. Likewise, it was known Walter's older sister, Polly, had also spent some years in Potton – and definite evidence of this we shall soon see.

With 'CJ's circumstances now radically different (arising from his marriage to Mary Anne as recently in 1880) – more favourable, to boot – from the previous occasion when consideration had had to be given to taking in one of his orphaned nephews and nieces, the clear advantages of this proposed arrangement were probably quickly perceived. Additionally, it was realised, Susannah would be best served by remaining in close proximity to some of her offspring and, in any case, the lady herself would have wanted that ... and, preferably, to be somewhere that was already known to her. But in her case a return to Potton (her late husband's once most settled home town) was out of the question – far too many memories of both happy and painful times there made it impossible to contemplate her living again in that town. Biggleswade, however, was a different matter: so close to Potton as to make it easy and convenient for 'CJ', at least, to pay regular visits to his mother, and already home to Susannah's other daughter and son–in–law, Susanna and Thomas Allen, not to mention the unmarried Anna Julia Hercock (Henry and Susannah's fourth daughter). Having gained general agreement for the carefully–hatched plan (probably formulated largely by 'CJ', Eliza and Susannah), it was settled – and the necessary moves put into effect.).

In the void left by Henry's death, clearly Susannah had had the greatest emptiness to fill. Her offspring helped her as far as they could, so having some of them, and with some grandchildren, too, living with her must have helped. But it would have been by taking her place in the local Baptist community that she would most quickly have been able to find her feet in this new, less comforting, world she now inhabited. Whilst she would have been comfortable in Nottingham with the Friends led by Mr. Coughtrey, her settling in Biggleswade would have required renewed effort to find her way in the Bedfordshire Baptist community from whom she'd been separated for some years since she and Henry had moved north.

We have no definite information, at present, about which Baptist Chapel Susannah Hercock (and her daughters) attached themselves to in Biggleswade or thereabouts. With the exception of Susanna, the wife of Thomas Allen (who had an unfortunate earlier history of involvement with this Chapel), none of them is mentioned in records of the Providence Baptist Chapel, Biggleswade (this gap in our knowledge is not helped by the fact that records for the Providence Chapel for the period 1884–1904 do not, apparently, survive). And, what little there is beyond the details of Susanna Allen's chequered history here is ambiguously unhelpful in that on 6th April 1884 a person of the surname 'ALLEN' was accepted into full membership at Providence, but no forename is given in the record of this event – so this probably was someone else entirely. (This unidentified person had been previously baptised – so it's unlikely to have been Thomas Allen because later evidence will show that he was still unbaptised as late as 1895; and it would not, of course, have been Susanna as she had been Baptised by her father long before her Membership had been transferred to Biggleswade from Potton in 1879.) Further, although, up to the end of 1884 the Pastor at the Providence Chapel was the Hercocks' old friend Mr. Richard Batchelor, he resigned from the post at the end of that year, citing difficulties over paying him the agreed salary but *'chiefly because there was neither peace nor order'* [From Mr. Richard Batchelor's resignation letter in 1884, as seen in the booklet **Providence Strict Baptist Chapel, Biggleswade, 150 years – 1843–1993**]. Once Susanna's mother and sister (Eliza) arrived in Biggleswade from Nottingham, some time in the mid– to late–1880s, and, presumably, expressed their intention of worshipping elsewhere than at Providence, Susanna and her husband may have opted to join with them. The mere fact of the earlier contretemps she'd had with the Chapel Elders makes it unlikely that Susanna Allen would have resumed worship there in later years, or that in its wake any other member of her wider family would have taken up attendance at Providence; but, in any event, the apparently unsettled atmosphere prevailing at the Providence Chapel (as evinced by its Pastor's resignation letter) would have been an effective deterrent to the Hercocks' becoming regular worshippers there notwithstanding their past good relations with Mr. Batchelor and others of the congregation.

Having studied all likely courses then open to them, I am of the opinion that the nearby Southill Chapel was, in fact, the most probable one to have attracted the 'HERCOCK' group now living in Biggleswade. Not only do we have the fact of Thomas Allen's 1880 marriage in this Chapel to Susanna Hercock, but – more significantly – the long–standing and much–loved Southill Pastor, Mr. John Warburton junior, was personally very well–known (along with his charming wife) to members of the 'HERCOCK' family. The Southill Chapel had become a Strict Baptist Chapel in the mid–1840s, under Mr. Warburton's guidance, and he had become a close ally and friend of Henry Hercock – the two of them had exchanged places in the pulpits on several occasions, as well as covering for each other. Although living in Biggleswade, the short journey to Southill would scarcely have presented an obstacle to the Hercocks' regular attendances there, for it is documented that other folk walked between the two places as a matter of course. Thus, although the Hercocks may, of course, now have attended somewhere else entirely, Southill is difficult to sweep aside on the evidence, even though the surviving records do not name members of the family. The absence of any 'HERCOCK' group family names in the records is not an insurmountable obstacle, as it would only have been folk who entered into membership that would have had their names recorded, and none of the 'HERCOCK' group may have taken such a step at Southill. For instance, excepting for the transfer of her Membership to Leeds (with Henry's), the Elder Susannah appears never to have become a member, solely on her own account, at any of the Baptist Chapels to which she gave her allegiance from time to time *after* she and Henry left Potton, and her namesake daughter may have decided not to try to revive her membership at Providence for eventual transfer to Southill. The real puzzle is with Eliza Jane, whose devout allegiance to the Cause had been so marked during her many years at Peterborough (where she'd lived with her parents) and Cirencester, but she, too, may have been biding her time during the sojourn at Biggleswade, undecided about the way forward then.

Information herein about the Southill Meeting House is from the **Further History of The Gospel Standard Baptists, Volume 3, 1958 – Some Midland and Eastern Counties Churches**, by S. F. Paul (hereinafter cited as '**S. F. Paul, 1958**'). This Meeting House had a history going back to the days of John Bunyan, when it was recorded in the **Bunyan Church Book** in the year 1697; Mr. John Warburton junior, already a celebrated Baptist Minister, held the Pastorate here from late in 1846. [**S. F. Paul, 1958**: Chapter II – Southill Chapel]

Writing from his home in the United States of America in 1931, Mr. John H. Dunkley, a former member of the Sunday School at Biggleswade's Providence Chapel during the 1880s recorded he '*of course attended chapel there when not walking over to Southill*'. [From the booklet **Providence Strict Baptist Chapel, Biggleswade, 150 years – 1843–1993**]

There is clear evidence that some individuals of the 'HERCOCK' group didn't always take the trouble to ensure their membership moved around from Chapel to Chapel with them. However, it was Henry who had instituted the transfer of his and Susannah's Joint Membership from Peterborough to Potton. Subsequently, there is the record in **The Church Book of Potton Baptist Chapel** of both of their Memberships being transferred to Leeds. There the trail ends for the time being, as no trace has been found to date of any possibly surviving records of the St. James' Street Baptist Chapel, Leeds – this being the Chapel at which Henry had been Minister.

Even with proceeds arising from the sale of Henry's **Memoir**, the widowed Susannah cannot have been particularly comfortably off financially, for Henry's estate was so inconsequential that no Will had been prepared which survived to enter the public domain ... whatever of his personal possessions and other assets he had, he must have stipulated their distribution verbally, or privately in writing, to those concerned. How, then, did she manage after he had gone?

Having reached her seventieth birthday on 15th August 1883, it's apparent Susannah will have relied in part on what little reserve of monetary assets Henry had been able to pass on to her, and what profits there were from the sale of his **Memoir**. But, for the rest, she will have depended on the generosity of certain of her family and Chapel Friends. It seems her principal family financial support came from the efforts of her daughters Eliza Jane and (probably to a lesser extent) Lucy Ann, during the time they all lived together at Nottingham where, it is presumed, one or both of these will have taken paid employment. Once

Susannah and Eliza had left Nottingham, though, it will have been up to Eliza almost entirely to earn sufficient to keep her mother – and this responsibility was such that a great deal of thought had gone into how it could be managed; there can be little doubt that 'CJ' will have contributed, too, but whether any others did is a moot point. In Biggleswade they had taken premises in Church Street which both suited their living requirements and provided accommodation for running a shop. Eliza had had the benefit of the best part of twenty years working as an Assistant to a Jeweller in his shop at Cirencester; now, with the wealth of that experience and knowledge to back her up, she felt confident in her own abilities in running her own business which she commenced in the Church Street location as soon as she'd been able to make all the necessary arrangements. Although, in order to buy herself some vital time to get fully organised, she may have continued in paid employment initially on coming to the town, it will not have been long before she was ready to open the doors of her own shop where she began selling Toys and Fancy Goods. This was a sensible line to choose at the time as the late Victorians had a particular penchant for such material possessions, and clock–work toys (which had started life in mid– 19th Century America) were becoming extremely popular.

Nearby in Potton, her brother Charles James, who had, of course, been in business on his own account for many years, and was making a notable success of his town–centre emporium which traded heavily in many of the sort of wares his sister was proposing to sell from her Biggleswade shop, was readily on hand with helpful advice and guidance, and probably was closely involved in helping get the Biggleswade enterprise off the ground.

Ruth Hercock as a toddler

The decade of the '80s was unrelentingly demanding for 'CJ', though the first few years, in particular, proved a frantically busy time for him, with several different, major commitments. As was only to be expected of him in his rôle of senior male member of the wider family. His contributions, too, to his mother's upkeep will have been a vital part of the equation, though he had his wife, Annie, and their own growing family to think of. 'CJ' and Annie had begun procreating with a daughter, Ruth, in May 1882. Had Henry Hercock not died when he did, this child of 'CJ's would have been the first grandchild for Henry from his then elder son, but the old man's death just a few months earlier, possibly marginally after the commencement of the pregnancy (but before it became known), had put paid to that. Ruth's birth was followed by those of Charles Ernest in 1883 and Edith in 1884.

Motherhood of three young children brought Annie an enormous physical and emotional burden to add to her already demanding daily routine around house and shop. Whilst 'CJ' shouldered the major share of the workings of their business, Annie invariably helped out as much as she could, often with the paperwork – we know this because her signature appears on at least one surviving bill issued in the 1890s by 'CJ' to Mr. A. Ginn, one of their regular customers in Potton. Also, according to the 1881 Census, they had a couple of paid employees. Moreover, in the late winter of 1885 additional assistance came to hand – in the person of 'CJ's niece Polly. Polly (her full name was Mary Ann Sawyer Hercock) was Walter's older sister; at the time of their becoming orphans on the deaths, in the 1870s, of their parents – William Henry Hercock and his wife, also Mary Ann – Polly had been despatched, after much heart–searching and difficult negotiations on the part of Henry and Susannah and others of her close relations, to an Orphanage in Bristol. Now, a few days before her seventeenth birthday, she was discharged from the Orphanage, whose authorities considered her unsuitable, on grounds of physical weakliness, to take a paid position. Hence her being despatched to Potton to her Uncle Charles! It was some twelve years

Orphanage Discharge Register Entry for Polly

since she'd previously lived here permanently with her parents and siblings (about half that time since her mother died and she and her brothers had been separated from each other), and things had changed a great deal since; as if making the adjustment to normal home life after some six–and–a–half years in the Orphanage wasn't enough of a challenge. One can imagine that, in the early days of her new situation, she'd have needed a great deal of comforting and reassurance, and her Aunt Annie – new on the scene here since Polly's previous stay – will have made every effort to keep the girl occupied so as to get her mind off unwelcome events of the past decade or so. Finding a suitable occupation was, naturally, not at all difficult, for Polly actually would have made a welcome, valuable addition to the household, able to help considerably with the young children and domestic chores. Perhaps she helped around the shop as well. Her fitting into family life with her Uncle, Aunt and cousins was further facilitated by the fact that she was a committed Christian, a Baptist at that, which would have gladdened the spirits of her new Guardians, making it somewhat easier for them to accommodate to her in this important aspect of their lives.

Gladdened, too, simply by the arrival in Potton that February of his sister, would have been Polly's brother Walter who had been keeping his head down with his studies ever since returning here. Now almost 15 years old, like his father before him Walter was mechanically–minded and revelled in getting his hands dirty! Fascinated by goings–on in his Uncle Charles' print–room, he must have been in there as often as possible, eager to help out with whatever small tasks could be entrusted to him. But his real interest lay in plumbing and all such allied matters, so it came as little surprise when he opted to follow an apprenticeship in this discipline. For now he was pleased to be re–united with his sister, and will have sat, agog, listening to all the tales she had to tell about life in the Orphanage and the children amongst whom she'd made her life these past years. And so it was that Polly entered afresh upon a normal life: she will gradually have come to cut a frequent sight around Potton's Market Place as she walked out with her young charges, or pushed the babies in a perambulator, or ran errands for her uncle and aunt. By the time Polly was happily settled in and enjoying her new life, she was fully ready to accept a further addition to the family occasioned by the birth of baby Bertram Hercock to her Aunt Annie the day after Christmas 1886.

On a less happy note, perhaps feeling somewhat left–out from all this family togetherness, Polly and Walter's youngest brother, Fred – who had also been an inmate in the Orphanage (he'd been recorded there at the 1881 Census, along with his sister), and was discharged in the mid–summer of 1886 – instead of being sent to live with any of his wider family, went straight to an apprenticeship in Leicester with a Joiner and Cabinet–Maker who was a complete stranger to the lad. Even Willy, the eldest of the orphaned offspring of William Henry and Mary Ann Hercock, was at least in the company of his grandparents and others on his late mother's 'SAWYER' side, at Peterborough – at the 1881 Census he was recorded there as an Apprentice Watchmaker; so poor Fred, the 'baby' of the pack, got the raw end of the deal all round.

The following year, 1887, saw great national and local celebration of Queen Victoria's achievement of 50 years on the throne, a milestone that was greeted with much rejoicing and carnival–like festivity across the land. At Potton there was a Committee set up to plan and oversee festive events – which included Sports for both adults and children, Bell–ringing, a Drum & Fife Band, Dancing to hired musicians – and the provision of food including baked potatoes. Several local tradesmen donated items to be given as prizes: for instance, Messrs. Fordham gave a barrel of ale, Mr. George Clarke gave ten pairs of boots, and Mr. C. J. Hercock gave an accordion. In addition to this, 'CJ' was a Subscriber (on whose subscriptions funding of the festivities depended) who gave ten shillings and sixpence – one of the more generous subscription amounts. Furthermore, 'CJ' printed various items relating to the celebrations, for which he was paid by the Committee two separate amounts of, respectively, £5 2s. 1d. (five pounds, two shillings and one penny) and 8s (eight shillings) for unspecified work, as well as £1 10s. 0d. (one pound and ten shillings) for 'balance sheets'. It will have been a busy year of printing for 'CJ' for it is known he also printed other items (for example, concert programmes [Photograph: see page C2]) concerned with the Golden Jubilee – and not just for purely Potton–based events. All this came on top of his normal workload of managing his town centre retail shop which serviced Potton's populace with their newspaper and magazine requirements in addition to supplying many other ordinary household goods.

> Information about the Potton Golden Jubilee celebrations, donations, subscriptions and payments comes from the Report & Financial Statement prepared for the Potton Jubilee Celebration in 1887 and (according to the document itself) printed by '*C. J. Hercock, Printer, Market Place, Potton*'. The original of this printed work survives in the Potton History Society Archives.

But this was also a year in which good friends and former Baptist colleagues of long standing died, bringing to the fore once more memories of the 'HERCOCK' clan's own great loss earlier in the decade. Amongst these, at Peterborough Henry Hercock's erstwhile friend at the North Street Baptist Chapel, William Henry Sawyer – the Hercock orphans' maternal grandfather – died on 4th August after a short, but very painful illness ... he was survived by his wife to whom a moving letter of condolence was sent from the Church Meeting at Chapel Street (to which he and his wife had transferred their allegiance some years after the Hercocks had left the city).

> The full text of the letter, and other relevant entries relating to William Henry Sawyer's death, are to be seen in **The Church Book of Salem Chapel, Chapel Street**, Peterborough. William Henry Sawyer's burial was in the Broadway Cemetery – the Burial Register Entry No. 8737 (in Register No. 4 covering Dec. 1880–Nov. 1889) gives this detail: Sawyer Henry William [*sic*] 79 years, Gentleman, d. 4th August, Eastfield Road, Peterborough, 2nd Division (unconsecrated) No. 383 "7 feet Deep Comm[n] Slabs", date of burial: 8th August, buried by whom: The Rev[d] F. Tryon, Signed: W[m] W. Flowers, Curator.
>
> I viewed the surviving grave slab, which is extraordinary large and had fallen on to its back, on 18th August 2009, and deciphered what I could of the heavily weathered inscription: it confirms that his widow and one of the couple's unmarried daughters (Alice Hannah Sawyer) lie in the same grave.

But possibly more difficult for the Hercocks to come to terms with was the death, just a few weeks later, of their old friend John Rowland Sturton, who had rendered the family such sterling service in one of their times of greatest need when he'd initiated, on the Hercocks' behalf, negotiations with the Bristol Orphanage. Now, though, his life was over and, most tragically, he'd survived his own father's death by just a whisker over two years. Both father and son died in Peterborough and, with their passing, the death knell of the Baptist Tabernacle in Westgate was sounded, for they had been its mainstays. And the old **Church Book** – which had begun its life in 1848 when the North Street Chapel at which it originally lived opened its doors, and which bore so many entries mentioning Henry Hercock, that Chapel's first Pastor – carried a poignant entry of the death of the Chapel's founder and most constant benefactor, John Sturton, who had also been constant friend to Henry. The three men mentioned hereinabove, who had stood large in the Hercocks' lives, were buried fairly near each other in Peterborough's Broadway Cemetery.

John Sturton died on 11th May 1885, a few days short of his 76th birthday; one of Peterborough's most respected citizens, he had, in addition to his involvement with the Strict Baptists, been prominent in various community positions in the city; he was survived by his widow and seven offspring. His son, John Rowland Sturton, died on 24th September 1887, aged 48 years (his and his father's large headstones are to be seen in prominent juxtaposition in one of the most highly sought–after locations in the Broadway Cemetery). William Henry Sawyer was buried in a grave also occupying a location of considerable prominence beside the Cemetery's central aisle and not far from the Sturtons'.

The Baptist Tabernacle, Westgate, Peterborough, finally closed in 1889 and the building was sold (it had been purchased from the General Baptist Trustees in 1879); the **Church Book** now was closed, too. Funds remaining after sale of the building and the discharge of all outstanding debts were donated to the Salem Chapel in Chapel Street, which was, thus, left to continue on its own of all the Particular Baptist Chapels in the city; this Chapel Street building was still in existence up to 1978 (when it was demolished after the Cause moved to Dickens Street).

Grave memorial of John Sturton,
Broadway Cemetery, Peterborough

† †

Up to, and continuing for a couple of years after, the time of Polly's coming to Potton to live with family, her other Uncle and Aunt – William and Mary Hayes Baxter – had also remained in the town, where William Baxter was pursuing his Tailoring business on the Market Place. They'd lived in Potton for in excess of ten years, a period which, it appears, was about the longest they liked to remain in any one place.

> Kelly's Directory of Bedfordshire, 1885, records the Baxters in Potton. Also, the Report & Financial Statement prepared for the Potton Jubilee Celebration in 1887, lists 'Mr. W. Baxter, Potton' as a Subscriber who contributed 10s 6d (ten shillings and sixpence) – this is presumed (with good reason to suppose it a near certainty) to have been Mary Hayes Baxter's husband. This latter sighting gives what is currently the latest–known dating of the couple in Potton.

Now they felt it was time to move on again. Following the demise of Mary's father (Henry Hercock), William and Mary had seen – and helped – their family successfully negotiate the delicate, winding path of life to the various points which all had now reached, with Mary's mother apparently settled in Biggleswade. So, at last Mary could think of herself and her husband in a more relaxed frame of mind, and attend to their own needs. Their decision to leave Potton, whilst naturally coming as a disappointing blow to other family members in the locality, was, nevertheless, one that all could understand, given what they knew of the couple's need to move at intervals to pastures new. William and Mary chose wisely in seeking out their new home – for, about 1888/89, they moved not many miles away,

William and Mary Hayes Baxter at Hitchin

to Hitchin in Hertfordshire, which had excellent rail links and, so, would allow them regular and rapid access to their wider family in the Potton and Biggleswade area. Ease of travel from Hitchin, much less than twenty miles to the south, was not the only prerequisite, of course, for – as was so important in the lives of many of their relations – an appropriate and suitable local place of worship was needed, too. As Hitchin then boasted a two Calvinistic Baptist Chapels, so their lives' most central requirements were evidently likely to be met by the town, in which they now settled to carry on their business. In branching out again into unknown territory of their new abode, they also now took on the new challenge of a different field in which to earn a living, leaving behind the Tailoring work that had been the couple's mainstay occupation for so many years. As with others in the family, it was to the Fancy Goods trade they now turned, running a retail shop from premises in Sun Street which was one of the town centre's quaintest and oldest shopping thoroughfares extending from the Market Place. One of the Strict Baptist Chapels – known as 'Mount Zion', in Park Street – had origins which went back to 1855 when a split occurred in the then extant Bethel Chapel (which had begun just five years earlier and was situated in Queen Street). It is not currently known which of these two Chapels the couple would have attended. Eager, too, to put to the test the increasingly popular art of posing for a studio photograph, the couple was photographed by T. B. Latchmore who owned a studio in the town.

> Kelly's Directories of Hertfordshire, 1890 and 1895, under the heading 'Places of Worship' in Hitchin, list: 'Calvinistic (Mount Zion), Park Street', and 'Calvinistic (Bethel), Queen Street'. Further information about both of these Chapels is from Mr. David J. Woodruff, Librarian of The Strict Baptist Historical Society, Dunstable, Bedfordshire. Records of neither Chapel have survived for the period embracing the Baxters' time in Hitchin.

There was one branch of the family of Henry and Susannah Hercock which was farther removed than any of the others from the centre of family life: Josiah Hercock and his entourage. At the 1881 Census the four of them – Josiah, his wife, Lucretia, and their two lads (John Henry and Ernest John Sydney) – were together in Whitstable, Kent, where Josiah was an Assistant in a Clothier's shop. No longer comfortable with his surname as it had been at the time of his birth and youth, Josiah had taken it upon himself to change it subtly, to 'HURLOCK'.

However, this was just the start of a completely new path into which he was to steer his life during the course of the ensuing few years, for he – then in his thirties – met and befriended an attractive young woman only just entering adulthood, and before long had started a scorching affair with her. From the outset, he was intent on no good, planning to desert his wife and the boys in favour of an illicit, second life with his new girlfriend who was a lass from Dereham, Norfolk. She was Nellie Emily Rix. That Josiah failed to mention to her his marriage and family, and the reality of his background, leaving the raunchy Nellie with the impression he was a fancy–free bachelor with no significant family ties, speaks volumes for his intentions right from the start. It was a deliberate act of deception, played out callously on his wife and teenage boys, and also with scant regard for his newfound lover with whom he must have been completely besotted almost from first sight. A trail of documentary dust and other, cunningly–planned devices implemented with deviously chilling efficiency soon hid him from Lucretia and his sons as he distanced himself from them and began elsewhere on his chosen new path with Nellie.

At the time all this intrigue was beginning, Josiah's 'HERCOCK' folk in Bedfordshire were unaware of his antics, busying themselves with rather more guileless ways of life in the provincial heartland. In Potton, Annie had given birth to another child, Albert, in 1888. At Biggleswade, Susannah will have taken fresh delight in her newest grandson – indeed, with 'CJ' living so close, the old lady was fortunate in having all her elder son's young brood on her doorstep, and they will have been frequent visitors to her home in Biggleswade where the little ones could, no doubt, be spoiled by their grandmother and aunts.

In the wider family arena, Henry Hercock's elder brother, William (to whom Henry had been quite close, sharing their Baptist faith), outlived Henry by some eight years, to reach an age measured as a decade longer than that of his late younger sibling; when he died, at Ketton, Rutland – where he and his second wife had lived a good many years – he was interred in a grave in the village's public cemetery. His impressively large headstone was inscribed:–

Grave memorial of Henry Hercock's elder brother, William

In affectionate remembrance of William Hercock, who departed this life October 11th 1889, aged 80 years. 'I know that my Redeemer liveth.'

I first visited the Town Cemetery at Ketton and discovered the headstone of William Hercock on 18th March 2009; the headstone was then in very good condition.

❖ ❖ ❖ ❖ ❖ ❖ ❖ ❖ ❖ ❖ ❖ ❖ ❖ ❖ ❖ ❖ ❖

Family Affairs in the 1890s

The Diversity of Henry Hercock's Family

By the time the decade of the 1880s ended, the family had seen the roughest edges of their emotions from the death of Henry smoothed somewhat, and had launched themselves into new channels which aimed to enable them to make the best of their own lives in the changed circumstances. When, therefore, the National Census was reached on 5th April

1891, all were in very different situations and/or geographical locations from a decade earlier. The coming decade, 'The Naughty Nineties' (as it became known), saw a significant relaxation in standards across the social spectrum, with further invasion of new ideas from the United States of America, though the seamier side of life will not have impacted the 'HERCOCK' clan in any great way, other than to give them further material over which to 'tut–tut' in conversation.

Spirits had risen considerably during the generally exceedingly mild February of 1891 when spring had come earlier than at any time in recorded English history, for the month was unique – being the driest then on record and, during the second half, seeing the temperature regularly approach (and occasionally surpass) 65° F (18° C) [From the 'Weather Watch' column of a Saturday issue of the **Daily Telegraph** in March 2009]. By now the confirmed 'HERCOCK' spinster, Eliza Jane, had seen her business in Biggleswade successfully through its teething stage to reach a degree of maturity that reflected her own inimitable style of flair and acumen in the management of her Toy– and Fancy–Goods shop in Church Street. Benefiting from her daughter's skillful mastery of her trade, the live–in mother, Susannah, could rest assured she was in good company – and had members of her settled, supportive family both on the spot and at nearby Potton; she was now recorded as 'living on own means' – the general euphemism employed for those who essentially didn't need to work to support themselves. Susannah's 13–year–old granddaughter, Ethel Eliza Duddington (from Peterborough), was here too, as Shop Assistant to her aunt Eliza, clearly gaining early–life experience in trade as well as giving company and help around the home and working environments. In adjacent Shortmead Street, Thomas and Susanna Allen now lived in retirement, having, perhaps, shut up shop around the time of Thomas' sixtieth birthday some years before; they were comfortably off.

Confirmation that Eliza Jane Hercock was living and working in Church Street, Biggleswade, before the time of the 1891 Census comes from Kelly's Directory of Bedfordshire, 1890, where there is recorded: '*Hercock Elizabeth (Mrs.), fancy shopkeeper, Church street*'. Although the lady's forename and marital status are not quite correct, there is no real doubt that this entry does actually relate to Miss Eliza Jane Hercock, for the 1891 Census data would otherwise be too much of a coincidence.

1891 Census for Biggleswade, Bedfordshire (Church Street): Head of Household: Hercock, Eliza J., Single, aged 49 years, Toy & fancy shop keeper (neither Employer nor Employed, occupying premises of 5 or more rooms), born Manton, Rutlandshire; also living in the household were Susanna [*sic*] Hercock (Mother, Widowed), and Ethel Duddington (Niece, Single).

Biggleswade was a busy, important market town and regional centre in those days (hub of the Biggleswade Poor Law Union), from which services for much of the surrounding area were provided; with a population that exceeded 5,000 people at the 1891 Census, the town was considerably larger than Potton (over 2,000). Its railway station, directly on the Great Northern line between London's King's

Cross station and the North via Peterborough (and, incidentally, passing through Hitchin to the south), gave it a distinct edge among other local settlements regarding wider communication links, and ensured an excellent postal service including four daily deliveries, the earliest of which was at 7.15 a.m. and the final at 6 p.m. (Sunday excepted). There were six assorted places of worship by 1890, including the Providence Baptist Chapel and a General Baptist Chapel. Southill, with a population (combined with three nearby hamlets) of over 1,200 souls at the Census, lay about 3½ miles south–west from Biggleswade and had its own railway station on the Bedford and Hitchin branch of the Midland Railway. Thus, Biggleswade was evidently an eminently suitable place for the 'HERCOCK' family members to live, providing Eliza Jane with a useful customer base for her retail trade in toys and fancy goods, and all the 'HERCOCK' clan a convenient and enriching centre for practising their religion, ease of travel to visit friends and relations in the vicinity or farther afield, especially at Potton, Peterborough and Hitchin, and familiar surroundings with which they were generally comfortable. Their life had, then, assumed an air of relative contentment and calm. But this was to be shattered early in the new decade, leading to a fresh upheaval.

Their Chapel Friends being so important to the Hercocks, it will have come as a considerable shock when the dear wife of their Pastor died in July 1891, heralding a period of great sadness. The Southill Chapel's **Church Book** records that '*The Church and Congregation, by her removal, had lost a true friend and peacemaker, and the Church a consistent member and a real Mother in Israel, by whom her loss was deeply lamented. Her mortal remains were interred in the Chapel Burying Ground on July 24, by William Bray of Stevenage, followed by most of her family and the members and congregation amidst much real sorrow.*' [**S. F. Paul, 1958**: page 70] Unfortunately, Mrs. Warburton's death was to prove apocalyptic for the Chapel insofar as it was the first stage of a dramatic change in prospects for the Friends. The second stage came just a few months later when the sorrowing widower, John Warburton, himself died on 19th January 1892. The Hercocks will have felt his passing very acutely, as will many others associated with the Chapel. '*He was a truly loving Pastor and father over his flock, to whom he was favoured to break the bread of life for upwards of forty–seven years, and was constantly administering to the various cases of the poor and needy of the congregation ; was of such a cheerful disposition, generous and kind to all around him, much given to meditation and prayer ; and the word preached, as many could testify, was in the demonstration of the Spirit, with power, unction, and savour,*' was how the Friends wrote of him in their **Church Book**. [**S. F. Paul, 1958**: page 71] Coming so soon after his wife's death, Mr. Warburton's own demise must have caused much consternation among the Friends – the 'HERCOCK' clan at Biggleswade would now be compelled to consider their longer–term futures once again, as their religious life was of greater importance to them than almost anything else, so deep was their faith and commitment to the Cause. It was undeniably synchronous that a short address at Mr. Warburton's funeral at Southill on 24th January was given by

Mr. Oldfield of Godmanchester, for it would not be long before the Hercocks were on the move again ... to Godmanchester, no less, to sit under Oldfield's Pastorate.

Tragedy having a habit of striking more than once in a defined area, it came to the Hercocks in Potton in a personal way about this time. 'CJ's and Annie's babies generally turned out to be strong, healthy infants, but the same did not apply to their next who was brought into the world, but died within a few days – in late September 1890; this unfortunate infant was not named. The poor mite's brief struggle to gain a hold on life, but inevitable death – occasioned by '*Premature Birth Atrophy and inability to take nourishment,*' (as the death certificate put it), over a period of three days – must have been most upsetting for all. The burial, in Potton's Town Cemetery, was the first and only 'HERCOCK' burial ever to take place there. In a show of support, it seems likely that 'CJ's elderly mother and some of his sisters came along for the simple funeral and interment. A year the following December, on Christmas Day of all days, Annie produced another child, Annie Christine, who – happily – thrived.

In other aspects, though, life prospered. Proof that trade in retail selling of Toys and Fancy Goods was both financially rewarding and personally satisfying to late Victorians came in the proliferation of such shops. The Hercocks clearly jumped on this particular bandwagon while the going was good. Following the lead given by her younger brother, 'CJ', in Potton, her younger sister, Eliza, in Biggleswade and the Baxters in Hitchin (now officially recorded at 16 Sun Street [Kelly's Directory of Bedfordshire, 1890: '*Baxter William, fancy repository, Sun street, Hitchin*'; also from the 1891 Census, which specifies the street address precisely]), the widowed Lucy Ann Underwood, who was still living in Nottingham with her three late–teenage or early–adult offspring, but had moved house to 46 York Street, had also ventured into dealing in Toys and Stationery, employing her elder daughter, Eliza Jane, as an Assistant. Lucy's son, William Henry, the next down in age, was, by the 1891 Census, serving an apprenticeship to an Iron Monger – later in the decade he went on to run his own business, dealing in 'smallware' – ironmongery, household goods, and other small items – from premises at 129 Carlton Road [Wright's Directory of Nottingham, 1898–99]. It is presumed the Underwoods still worshipped at the Chaucer Street Chapel under Mr. Coughtrey. Lucy Ann was to continue here in Nottingham throughout most of the decade of the '90s, as Proprietor of her Toy Shop – the income from which probably provided her mainstay financial support.

> 1891 Census: '*Lucy Ann Underwood, 46 York Street, Nottingham, Toy Dealer (Employer)*'.
> Wright's Directory of Nottingham, 1891: '*Underwood Mrs. Lucy Ann, toy dealer, 46 York st*'.
> Kelly's Directory of Nottinghamshire, 1891: '*Underwood, Lucy Ann (Mrs.), stationer, 46 York street*'.
> Wright's Directories of Nottingham, 1893, 1894-95, 1896–97: '*Underwood Mrs. Lucy Ann, toy dealer, 46 York st*'.

Meanwhile, at Peterborough the 'DUDDINGTON' clan was thriving. Joseph and Helen had six offspring so far to their names, all living at home which was 'Olive House', in Walpole Street; this home had already given them shelter for a good many years, and was yet to continue to do. Joseph was working as an employed Joiner; their eldest son, Joseph Charles Henry, as a Grocer's Assistant; the next, Alfred, as a Corn Merchant's Clerk; three of the younger children were at School, and the youngest, Eva, was but 2 years old. Joseph and Helen – Helen was Henry and Susannah Hercock's youngest surviving daughter – continued to add to their brood and, some time in the middle of the decade, sat with them all for a splendid group photograph of the whole family. Ranging from the eldest, Joseph Charles Henry (then about 23 years of age), to the youngest, Vernon Leslie (about 4 years), the offspring were nicely grouped around their proud parents who sat next to each other for the photographer; the photograph appears to have been taken in the garden of their Peterborough home.

The entire Duddington family, circa 1895
Standing, left to right: Susanna Mary, Joseph Charles Henry, Anna Julia Helen,
Alfred William, Ethel Eliza, Cecil Ernest;
Sitting, centre: Joseph, Helen Letitia (née Hercock)
Sitting, on the ground: Eva, Vernon Leslie

Helen did her familial duty by temporarily housing her older sister, Anna Julia, on the occasion of the 1891 Census; Anna perhaps repaid her sister and brother–in–law by helping out around house with some of the younger children. But there is documentary evidence to confirm that this simpleton of a daughter of Henry and Susannah ordinarily lived in Biggleswade with her widowed mother and the others around the 1890s.

By mid–November 1890, the maverick Josiah's sweetheart, Nellie, was some 4 months' pregnant, so he had this as motivation to get on and marry her. Craftily concealing the true facts of his earlier life, Josiah – who had introduced himself to Nellie in the first instance as 'John Hurlock' – now sustained, augmented and reinforced his deception to make it appear he was entirely eligible to marry the single young woman whose charms had so beguiled him. Using the relatively greater anonymity that a licence would afford him in his bigamous union, he arranged the wedding for Sunday, 16th November 1890. Whereas he was then living in Pinner Road, Bushey, Hertfordshire, the marriage ceremony was held in the distant Parish Church of St. Luke, Old Street, Middlesex, which meant it was registered in the Holborn District, deep in the central London commercial area. His bride, like himself a Draper's Assistant – probably indicating the pair had first met through work – was said to be a spinster of Churchill House in Chiswell Street; she was 24 years of age, against Josiah's 38 years (this was actually the correct age for his true–life birth year). Using his alias of 'John Hurlock', and the quasi–genuine name of 'John Henry Hurlock' for his supposed father (whom he correctly identified as a deceased Baptist Minister), and ensuring none of his blood relations attended the wedding, Josiah successfully pulled off this escapade – which must have been much to his relief. Early the following year, in his information given to the Census Enumerator, Josiah left a trail of further evidence of how he concealed his true identity in that he cited his birthplace as 'Leicester'. He must have been a cool customer for his wife and her relations not to have smelled a rat sufficient to call Josiah's identity into question. Whether anyone at all ever wondered about him we shall probably never know. Cleverly, his choice of alias meant that such personal items as cufflinks, which could have carried his initials 'J. H.', or a monogram based on them, held true, thus enabling him to use long–held items like these to bolster his false identity whilst simultaneously retaining some of his most favoured personal possessions. But his apparent separation from most, if not all, relations must surely have raised questions in the minds of his new wife's family. Were they naïvely unsuspecting, or did the wily Josiah brush aside probing questions with deft astuteness?

Following the marriage, the couple set up home at 59 Queen's Road, Watford, Hertfordshire, where the expected child was born on 30th March 1891. The baby, a girl, was registered almost four weeks later by the father who then declared her name as 'Nellie Hurlock'. However, at the Census just a few days following the birth (that is, some three weeks before the registration was made), the baby was named as 'Dorothy M. Hurlock' – and stated to be 1 month old (the true age was at most 1 week). The family did not remain long at Watford, however, for by 1894 they had moved to 15 Balfour Terrace, High Road, Leytonstone, Essex, where (in June) Nellie bore Josiah–John (see below) another girl whom they named Dora May Hurlock – this choice highlights an obvious change of mind the couple had, for some reason, over the first child's name. Whilst remaining in Leytonstone, they soon moved again, however, this time to an High Road address itself.

> To avoid ambiguity, from this point onwards (except where the context requires otherwise and makes clear to whom reference is being made) I shall refer to Josiah Hercock or Hurlock *alias* John Hurlock as 'Josiah–John Hurlock', or simply 'Josiah–John'.
>
> It appears their first address on the High Road was at Number 700 (as this is what is recorded in Kelly's London Suburban Directory, Northern Parts, for 1896); however, by April 1897 they were living at 696 High Road, Leytonstone. Either they'd moved a few doors along or some re–numbering of premises in High Road had taken place.

They went on to have their first boy, John Frederick (in later life he was more often to be known as 'Frederick John', often shortened to 'Fred'), whose birth was registered early in 1896; then a second, Victor Rex, who was born on 26th April

Victor Rex (left) and John Frederick Hurlock, circa 1900

1897; and a third, Henry Ernest, during 1899. If any child born into a family were to be a harbinger of ill fortune, then this latest probably was that child, for he was to die of pneumonia on the very first day of the New Year, 1900, and the family's circumstances just a few years farther on from this unhappy event were to become dire.

Josiah–John Hurlock cared nothing, presumably, for the legitimate family whom he had dumped when he took up with Nellie Rix. Lucretia and her two sons must have found the going hard, for Lucretia will have had to find the means to provide for all of them – perhaps relying on her wider family and some friends, as well as whatever Church or Local Municipal handouts could be gleaned. In the early 1890s they were living – somewhat ironically, given their impoverished circumstances – at 22 Goldsmith Street, Nottingham. Lucretia, probably

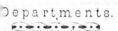

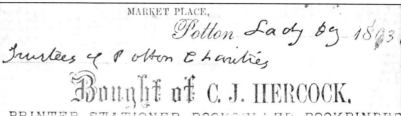

Departments.

PRINTING.
ry description of Letterpress Printing
ne upon the premises. Lithographic
d Copperplate to order.

STATIONERY.
paper in five quire packets at 4½d. 6d
. 1s. and 1/6. Envelopes 6d, 8d, 10d,
ne, Terra Cotta, Pink, Grey, Ivy leaf
al a variety of fancy patterns of Note
per and Envelopes to match; the new
urt Mourning Paper, & Black bordered

INK.
len's & Hyde's, in 1d, 3d, 6d, 1/- and
s bottles.
usual variety of stationery sundries.

BOOKBINDING
in a superior manner, and with des-
h.

PAPERHANGING
in stock, and hung by superior work-
-n.

HABERDASHERY
LS, Berlin, single and double, and a
riety of shades in each color; Fin-
rings in an assortment of colors and
alities. Fleecy, Andalusian, Shetland
chive, Sicilian, German Knitting Yarn
celsior Soft Spun, Ice Wool, etc.

Needles, Buttons, Tapes. Trimm-
gs, Lace, and a general variety too
merous to mention.

TON, Arden's Crochet in 1d, and 2d,
lls; and Knitting at 1/6 per lb.

Lee Sewing Cotton 100 yds. 2 for 1½d.
Red for marking, M min 4, etc.

TOYS.
rge stock kept, which is being con-
ntly renewed.

NEWS.
arcel down every morning of London
aily Newspapers. Weekly Papers and
onthly Periodicals to order.

FANCY GOODS.
ums, Writing Desks and Cases, Needle
ases, Pincushions, Inkstands, Work-
oxes, Silk-lined Baskets Blotters, Vases
ew China, Ladies and Gents Dressing
ases and Bags, Ornaments, Photo
rames, Glove & Handkerchief Boxes,
apier-machie Trays and Brackets,
urses, Wallets etc.

BOOKS.
rge stock of Reading Books from 4d.,
v & - Cloth bound. Wesleys, Congrega
ional and Gadsby's Hymns.

mns Ancient and Modern, Book of
ommon prayer; and both in 1 vol, or in
lip Cases. Birthday Text Books etc.

SMOKING.
pes, all prices; in cases from 1/6 each
Cigar & Cigarette cases and Holders,
Pouches, Vesuvians, Wax Vestas, and
other Smoking requisites.

MUSIC.
olins and Fittings of all kinds, Concer-
tinas, Accordians, etc.

Detail from a bill issued in 1893 by Charles James Hercock

unaware of exactly what had happened to her husband Josiah, informed the Enumerator at the 1891 Census that she was 'married', and a 'wife' – at least this could avoid some awkward questions about her having the two males living in. Her elder boy was working as a Ledger Clerk, whilst the younger was an Insurance Clerk – both locally.

Elsewhere in the wider family, prosperity on a modest scale enabled folk to pursue their daily lives in unpretentious comfort, as was the 'HERCOCK' way. 'CJ' and Annie had successfully transformed his elder brother William Henry's former retail business into a bustling centre of activity, making it one of the foremost shops on Potton's Market Square. Although most Trade Directory listings of the 1880s and 1890s record him as a Stationer and News–Agent, his shop stocked an extraordinary diversity of domestic and commercial goods, causing 'CJ' himself to continue to call it a 'Fancy Repository' (as several Trade Directories of earlier years had done). Even so, the variety of the enterprise is somewhat concealed by this term, for he offered such services as Printing and Bookbinding, sold a vast range of Stationery items, Newspapers, Magazines and Books, Paperhangings (wall–paper), Wools and Haberdashery, Toys and Giftware, and many other items including some dry provisions such as packeted tea–leaves. And, as a small–time Printer, 'CJ' was able to satisfy many of the town's and local environs' requirements for posters, leaflets and flyers, booklets, and a host of other, small–scale printed material, including such things as memo pads and account books, from his print–room behind the shop. The work was, obviously, hugely demanding and tiring, requiring 'CJ' to have regular, full–time employees (whereas the 1881 Census had specified how many, from 1891 onwards the number of employees was not recorded), but also brought its considerable rewards – both monetary and in satisfaction – so that the family established themselves with an enviable standard of living in the town, with a comfortable home of capacious proportions dominating the local scene and skyline around Potton's trade, social and cultural centre ... the Market Place. For a time 'CJ' also acted as the local agent for the British and Foreign Bible Society.

> Kelly's Directory of Bedfordshire, 1898, under the heading 'Commercial': 'British & Foreign Bible Society Depôt, Market pl, Potton (Charles James Hercock, agent)'.

There can be little doubt that 'CJ' will have contributed a generous amount to his mother's upkeep. 'CJ's three oldest children were probably settled in the Potton Board School; and, as a family they worshipped in the Baptist Chapel, continuing the tradition of 'HERCOCK' involvement there which had now well exceeded twenty years. Somehow, they had learned not to allow themselves to be haunted by the ghost of 'CJ's father, Henry, peering down at them from the Chapel's pulpit! As Baptists do not generally have young children baptised (christened), there is very little documentary evidence of the active involvement of the family, as now constituted, in the Potton Baptist Chapel, but a record of the acceptance into full communion of the Chapel of 'Mrs. C. Hercock' in December 1894 provides a vital clue.

> Information from **The Church Book of Potton Baptist Chapel** – the full entry reads as follows:– 'On the first Lords Day in Dec.ʳ 1894, Mʳ Smith · Pastor gave the right hand of fellowship to Mʳˢ C. Hercock – and she was received into full communion – Mʳˢ Hercock had been previously baptized – (some time before coming to reside here) she said she was a partaker of grace at the time – though that church was not of the same order–'.

> It is not known at which other Baptist Chapel Annie had been baptised, but she was living at Fletton (near Peterborough) and aged about 14 years at the 1871 Census; and, as she was about 16 years old when baptised (as we shall later find), it is most likely to have been in or near Fletton. From a much later date (1908), even more definite evidence will be seen to corroborate the identity irrefutably.

On the first Lords Day in Decr 1894.
Mr Smith Pastor gave the right hand
of fellowship to Mrs C Hercock, and
She was received into full communion —
Mrs Hercock had been previously baptized —
(Some time before coming to reside here)
She said She was a partaker of grace at the
time — though that church was not of Same order —

Potton Baptist Chapel Church Book extract, 1894

'CJ' and Annie's relatively secure, settled way of life on the Market Place was to be shattered during hours of darkness one deep winter's night in January 1897. Unbeknown to the building's occupants as they slept, a lump of fallen, glowing soot lay smouldering in contact with some old woodwork which eventually burst into flame – and fire quickly caught hold. 'CJ', asleep in the bedroom above, was the first to be aroused by crackling sounds and, having quickly established that a large part of the shop premises below was alight, gave the alarm and supervised the evacuation of the building; he and Annie and some of the older children led the younger ones, still in their nightwear – through smoke and flaming darkness filling the shop – to safety. It was the early hours of the morning, but the local Volunteer Fire Brigade was summoned and was able to extinguish the fire in time to save the greater part of the building, though the shop had been extensively damaged and most of the stock ruined by burning, smoke or water. The family lost greatly from this tragedy as insurance premiums had not been maintained at sufficient levels to bring a full payout by the two insurance companies concerned. This meant that, in order to restock the shop, 'CJ' had to dig deep into the family's financial reserves which became so heavily depleted that his and Annie's aspirations for their future were to be seriously altered.

> Ruth, Charles James Hercock's eldest child, was so mentally scarred by this incident (which happened when she was in her sixteenth year) that thenceforth she had a fear of fire. In later life, as Ruth Flowerday, she was to recount the tale of her experience that night to her children, one of whom was to become my father, telling it so vividly it was as if she was then reliving the terror of it all.

My father also told me that, as much of the stock – such as knitting wools – had been damaged by smoke, even though not completely destroyed, the insurance company refused to cover its value despite it being unsaleable. A newspaper account of the fire describes it in graphic detail – and appeared in **The Biggleswade Chronicle, Sandy, Potton and Shefford Times** of 23rd January 1897 (a copy of the account survives in the Potton History Society Archives).

Despite this severe setback, 'CJ' and Annie picked themselves up and got on with their lives as best they could. Perhaps bringing some cheer to their downcast spirits, Annie fell pregnant again in the spring, and gave birth in November. Thus, their last–born child, Wilfred Henry, may well have been unplanned; he, too, went on to survive infancy ... and actually quickly became his mother's favourite. By the time of his birth, his eldest sister, Ruth, was a 'Pupil–Teacher' at the town's Board School where she had made a close friend of another girl of about her own age: Alice Mary Woodman (from another local Baptist family of stalwarts at the Potton Chapel), who also joined the staff of the School in the same capacity, though (unlike Ruth) Alice was not to go on to teach in later life.

Both Polly and Walter were spared the horrors of the fire as they had parted company with their Potton relations before it happened; thus, at the 1891 Census Mary Ann had taken work In Service with a Grocer at Chipping Barnet, Hertfordshire, whilst Walter – then living in Wanstead, Essex – was working as a Plumber for a local man, and lodging locally. Their youngest brother, Fred, had given up his apprenticeship, not having taken to the carpentry and joinery trade, and was also then living in Wanstead where he, too, was in lodgings (though not with his brother). Having completed his apprenticeship with his 'SAWYER' grandfather in Peterborough, even the eldest orphan, William Henry, had moved to Essex – he, perhaps, had been the forerunner of the pack – and, yet unmarried, was employed as a Jeweller's Assistant in Romford (where he lodged). With a promising future in this trade, his young life was cut cruelly short, though, at the end of 1897 when he died of leukaemia (as recorded on the death certificate – though this is not mirrored in a published newspaper report, below) from which he'd been suffering for many months. His sister Polly, still a single woman, had gone to live with him in Romford to care for him during his final days, and he'd made a Will in March leaving his entire Estate to her. However, he'd taken himself to Margate, Kent, which is where he died (in a special hospital) just a few days before Christmas, casting great glumness over not only his siblings, but also many other members of his extended 'HERCOCK' and 'SAWYER' families. His body was transported back home, and on 28th December was interred in a grave in the town's cemetery at Romford, witnessed by many sad relatives and friends.

A satin–lined fob–watch box bearing the inscription: '*W. H. Hercock ... Watchmaker and Jeweller High Street Romford*' eventually found its way into the possession of his great–niece Mollie Barbara, who has it to this day. [Photograph: see page C4]

The following announcement was published locally in a Romford newspaper:–

DEATH OF MR. W. H. HERCOCK.

We regret to announce the death of Mr. W. H. Hercock, jeweller, of High–street, which took place early yesterday morning at Margate, where he had, for some months past, been staying in the hope of benefiting his health. Mr. Hercock had undergone six or seven operations for tuberculosis, the first being performed about eighteen months ago. The disease, however, became aggravated, and, establishing itself in the lungs, caused pulmonary consumption, from which death occurred. Mr. Hercock, who was barely thirty years of age, came to Romford from Peterborough, and for about eight years was assistant to Mr. W. B. Lake, whom he succeeded in the business on Mr. Lake's retirement in April, 1894. Of a quiet, unassuming disposition, Mr. Hercock had won the regard and esteem of his fellow townsmen and all with whom he was brought into contact, and his untimely death will be received with genuine regret.

[The foregoing is a facsimile transcription from the original newspaper clipping dated 22nd December 1897]

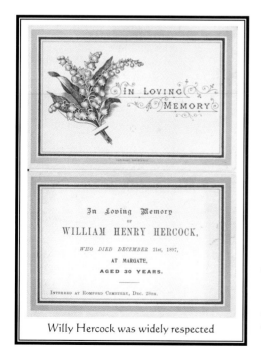

Willy Hercock was widely respected

Willy's absence will have been sorely felt at the marriage the following March of his brother, Walter, to Edith Alice Abrams, a 21–year–old local girl, in Romford's Trinity Wesleyan Church to which Walter, after having been brought up a Strict Baptist, had switched his allegiance – a notable, but then rare, break with the faith of his parents. Among the witnesses to the signing of the Register was their youngest brother, Fred Hercock.

Meanwhile, at Hitchin fortune seems to have been smiling on the 'BAXTER' couple whose retail business in the town's Sun Street was booming in the mid–1890s. They'd added Glass– and China–ware to their range of quality merchandise on sale. As several other members of the family were involved in a similar trade around the time, it would seem probable that they all exchanged information about promising

THE FRUITS OF HIS LABOURS

product lines, suppliers, pricing and other related matters. So far as earning their livings was concerned, they appear to have found their niche, with a particularly profitable seam to work. Should it have appeared that – due to their being a little out on a limb in the geographical sense – the twosome was somehow no longer centrally involved in affairs of their wider family, events of the mid–1890s would unquestionably prove otherwise. For, irrefutably catalysed by the death, in 1892, of Pastor John Warburton at Biggleswade, within a few years the Allens and the Hercocks from that town together with the Baxters from Hitchin all relocated to Godmanchester where the Particular Baptist Chapel then had their friend Mr. Joseph Oldfield as its Pastor. (Thomas Allen handed over his Grocery business in Shortmead Street to his son Joseph).

> Kelly's Directories of Hertfordshire, 1894 & 1895, under the heading 'Commercial': 'Baxter William, fancy repository & glass & china dealer, Sun street, Hitchin'.
> Kelly's Directory of Bedfordshire, 1898: 'Allen Joseph, grocer, Shortmead street, Biggleswade'.

◉ ◉ ◉ ◉ ◉ ◉ ◉ ◉ ◉ ◉ ◉ ◉ ◉ ◉ ◉ ◉ ◉ ◉

They put their Faith in Godmanchester

This mass migration of family members appears to have begun some time during early 1894; those involved settled in their new location within a couple of years of each other, arriving in two distinct groups. The first group, including Susannah and her two unmarried daughters, Eliza Jane and Anna Julia, moved into a house in Godmanchester's Post Street to share it; the choice of premises was such that Eliza could conveniently carry on her business which now was principally to do with selling Toys. Anna assisted in the Shop, and both these ladies, now in their mid–fifties, shared the responsibility of caring for their mother (now in her eighties). Thomas and Susanna Allen similarly lived in Post Street – in a nearby property. Indeed, it would seem that all these folk had selected the two properties which lay just a few doors from each other and had become available more or less at the same time. The Baxters, too, appear to have moved into an abode in Post Street, being the second group to arrive in the town (probably early in 1896), but whether they started off by sharing with some of the other family folk, or had a separate residence of their own, is uncertain. At any rate, the entire assemblage was clustered geographically – and all because they had a common desire to join together in celebration of their religion and to worship at the Godmanchester Particular Baptist Chapel.

There was also in these 'HERCOCK' sisters' coming together in this way – which was the first time they'd all lived in such close proximity since the days of the girls' youth in Lincolnshire (the family had had about two years in Spalding during Henry Hercock's attachment to the Ebenezer Chapel there) or, perhaps, in early adulthood at Peterborough – an acceptance of their common responsibility to care for their ageing and increasingly frail mother. She'd now lost most of her teeth, which resulted in her lower face having the graceless sunken, wizened appearance so typical of the condition; and was probably also showing other ravages of time. That her eldest and three other of her daughters were sufficiently concerned to be willing to live with, or very near, their mother is testament to their caring togetherness approach, allowing them to share both the burden of care and joys of living with such an esteemed elder. So it was, then, that the greatest, most significant, of family rearrangements since that which had taken place in the immediate aftermath of Henry Hercock's death some fifteen years earlier was accomplished.

Godmanchester Particular Baptist Chapel's records have preserved some of the Hercocks' involvements for us, though – as had been the case elsewhere – Susannah, Henry's widow, appears not to have become a formal member. Nor did Anna Julia make that commitment.

First of the group to be named in the Chapel records is Thomas Allen, for at a Special Church Meeting held on 19th May 1895 we read that 'Mr Oldfield proposed Mr Thos Allen as a candidate for Baptism & Church Membership which was carried. Friends Pack & Ilett were appointed to visit him'. [Godmanchester Strict Baptist Church Book, 1882–1947: page 77] Susanna, his wife, soon followed: on 23rd June another Special Church Meeting was held, and on this occasion 'Mr Oldfield proposed Mrs T Allen for Church Membership who had been sitting down with us at the Lords table for about 15 months. Friends Dighton & Peacock were appointed to visit her'. [Ibid.] Given that Susanna had clearly put behind her the kerfuffle over her non–attendance at Communion at Providence Chapel, Biggleswade, this is proof of her continuing commitment to the Cause and suggests she had been worshipping elsewhere in the years prior to arriving at Godmanchester – although it has to be observed that, as her Membership was not being transferred from elsewhere, it may have lapsed wherever previously it

had been held. Since it is known she had had her original Membership at Potton, and that was transferred to the Providence Chapel in Biggleswade in 1879, it looks as if she had not taken the trouble to resurrect it anywhere else prior to coming here to Godmanchester – which could account for there being no record of her Membership at the Southill Chapel (if, that is, she'd been attending there). As she had been taking Communion here in Godmanchester since about March of 1894, it is safe to conclude that she may have begun attending the Chapel shortly before then – which gives a hint of the earliest likely time of moving to the town from Biggleswade, evidently as the forerunner (with her husband) of the whole family cluster.

Verbatim passages from **Godmanchester Strict Baptist Church Book, 1882–1947** are reproduced by kind permission of The Gospel Standard Baptist Library, courtesy of Miss Marion G. Hyde (Librarian).

The Pastor, Mr. Oldfield, must have thought highly of the 'HERCOCK' folk, for at this same meeting at which he put forward

Susanna Allen's name it is recorded that '*Mr Oldfield also proposed Miss Hercock sister of the above & Friends Chandler & Brighty were appointed to visit her*'. [*Ibid.*]

Godmanchester Chapel's Quarterly Church Meeting was then not far off, so these proposals were deliberate and particularly timely. When the date, 30th June 1895, of the Meeting arrived, the formal decisions seem to have been readily reached, for the '*Visitors having reported favourably of ... Mrs Allen Miss Hercock & Mr Allen, they each came before the Church and gave a very satisfactory account of the Lords dealings with them & were unanimously received by the Church*'. [*Ibid.*] 'Susanah' [*sic*] Allen's name was entered on the Membership List, immediately followed by that of her sister Eliza Jane Hercock, on 7th July; Thomas Allen's name was added on 4th August – as the formal process of becoming a Chapel Member was undertaken during a Service of Sunday worship, these dates were both Sundays. [**Godmanchester Strict Baptist Church Book, 1882–1947**: Membership List, page 15] As Thomas Allen was the only one of the three to undergo Baptism at this time, this accounts for his separate induction.

This gives us no clue as to the real timing of Eliza's arrival in the town, but it's a safe assumption that she, too, will have attended the Chapel for some little while before deciding on a formal Membership; again, some time during the early part of 1894 would seem to be indicated. She was still

Joseph Oldfield

evidently trading at Biggleswade during 1893 (or even very early 1894) as the Bedfordshire Directory for 1894 lists her there (though information for this edition would have been collected the year before and is not, therefore, a chronologically accurate indication of her continuing presence in that locality); but the Huntingdonshire Directory for 1898 shows her running her Toy Repository at Godmanchester.

Having removed to Godmanchester, Thomas Allen now resumed his shop–keeping activity as recorded in the Kelly's Directory of 1898. Quite why, at about 70 years of age, he took up work again is a mystery, but it may be an indication that he felt the need to add to his financial reserves in order to ease the burden of contributing towards providing care for his mother–in–law. Of course, there was the consideration that the premises in Godmanchester may not have been economical to rent, for the couple was occupying a substantial property which had more than five principal rooms.

> Kelly's Directory of Bedfordshire, 1894, under 'Commercial': 'Hercock Elizabeth (Mrs.), fancy shopkeeper, Church street, Biggleswade'. [Comment has previously been made on errors in a similar, earlier entry and the reality of her name and marital status]
>
> Kelly's Directory of Huntingdonshire, 1898, under 'Commercial': 'Hercock Eliza Jane (Mrs.), toy repos'. [See the note above]
>
> Kelly's Directory of Huntingdonshire, 1898, under 'Commercial': 'Thomas Allen, shopkeeper'.

The Baxters came from Hitchin some time after all these others. At a Special Church Meeting in Godmanchester Chapel, held on 3rd March 1897, it is recorded that 'The Pastor proposed Mr & Mrs Baxter for Church Membership. After sitting down with us for more than a year they felt desirous to unite with us. Friends Dighton & Pack were appointed to visit Mr Baxter & Toseland & Chandler to visit Mrs Baxter'. [Godmanchester Strict Baptist Church Book, 1882–1947: page 81] A little under three weeks later, at a Quarterly Church Meeting held on 21st March, the record shows that 'Visitors reported favourably of Mr & Mrs Baxter & they each came before the church & gave a very good account of the Lords gracious dealings with their souls & were unanimously received'. [Ibid.: page 82] Subsequently, the Chapel's Membership List shows their names were first entered (one following the other) on 4th April 1897, as 'William Baxter' and 'Mary Baxter'. [Godmanchester Strict Baptist Church Book, 1882–1947: Membership List, page 15] These details, if a reasonably accurate record of the length of time the Baxters had been worshipping at the Chapel, suggest they moved to Godmanchester early in 1896 or even possibly late in 1895 (though it seems unlikely they would have missed the opportunity of picking up the busy Christmas–period trade in Hitchin and would, on balance, have deferred removal until the slack month of January 1896). However, although the couple made their home in Godmanchester, it was not here that they set up their business; instead, they chose adjacent, larger, Huntingdon – just a short walk away – for the siting of their Fancy Repository at 3 George Street – at this time William was about 58 years of age, Mary about 60 years. It appears they were still quite sprightly, sufficiently so for them to be able to walk the short distance between their Shop and home, enjoying a gentle stride beside the River Ouse for a good portion of the way – this walk would have encompassed the raised causeway leading to Huntingdon bridge, thence to the town centre of Huntingdon.

> Kelly's Directory of Huntingdonshire, 1898, lists William Baxter as a Private Resident at Godmanchester; and, under the heading 'Commercial', operating his 'fancy repository' at Huntingdon.

Godmanchester, site of an important ancient Roman settlement, was quite a small place (with a population of about 2,000), Huntingdon the far larger and grander of the two (with a population more than double that of Godmanchester), so living in the former and trading at the latter made good sense. Godmanchester was an inland port in those days (the sea outlet of the River Ouse is into The Wash at (King's) Lynn, Norfolk), with a charter granted to the borough by King John in 1213 ... this remained in force until the town was incorporated as a Municipal Borough in 1835. At around the time of the arrival of the 'HERCOCK' group, the town was governed by a Corporation of which some of the elected members were among the committed Friends of the Particular Baptist Chapel. In comparison, Huntingdon (also significant in Roman times), situated on the left bank of the Ouse, was the County Town and, as such, centre of many civic amenities and services for both itself and the surrounding area as well as the entire County. It, too, had been granted a charter by King John, and was similarly incorporated as a Municipal Borough in 1835. Huntingdon was an important military centre for the Royalists during the English Civil War, but was at least once taken by the Parliamentary Army. Its importance in this connection may have had something to do with the fact that the town was a stronghold of the 'CROMWELL' family: the baptism (christening) of Oliver Cromwell is to be found in the Register of St. John's Church, in 1599, he allegedly having been born in a house sited on land which had come into the hands of his family after previously having been in the possession of an Order of Austin Canons who had had their priory in the vicinity. Whilst Huntingdon may have been a good choice to conduct business, from the Hercocks' point of view it could never have been their choice of place to live or worship; for, by stark contrast to Godmanchester, it did not have a Particular or Strict Baptist Chapel, and, indeed, at the time the only Baptist Chapel in Huntingdon was unified with the Congregationalist cause. Both towns had excellent railway links, based on their own stations, which meant the Hercocks could easily travel to visit more distant relations who, in turn, could come to see them. A continuation of the main road from Huntingdon, Post Street – where several of the group elected to set up home – was where one would have found oneself immediately after crossing the river bridge from Huntingdon: part of the major thoroughfare through the centre of Godmanchester. Soon, swinging round to the left as it proceeded past the Town Hall, it became East Street (also known as Cambridge Street). It was with the latter that St. Ann's Lane, a back street a little to the south, ran more or less parallel.

It is fortunate (for us) that some of the Hercocks took up membership of the Godmanchester Chapel, for its surviving records give us a good picture of who was in the town, and roughly when. On the one hand, because neither Anna Julia nor her mother is named in the Chapel's **Church Book**, it is impossible, on the face of it, to say exactly when these two will have moved to the town. On the other hand, so far as Susannah Hercock is concerned, her arrival will without doubt have coincided with that of her other daughter, Eliza Jane – so some time early in 1894 is most probable. Anna probably arrived then, too, as she was at once so inextricably involved with her mother's care and herself dependent on her more able, older sister's general supervision, financial provision and overarching family management. That none of the whole cluster had Chapel Membership transferred from elsewhere points to the fact that their respective memberships had either lapsed, or were never established, in the immediately–preceding Baptist communities where they'd lived prior to arriving in Godmanchester. In Eliza's case, this is further evidence that she'd probably been in Nottingham for some time after leaving Cirencester (where her Membership was previously held).

What, then, do we know of the town's Particular Baptist Chapel and local community of the Cause, and what can we deduce about why it held such magnetic attraction for the Hercocks? Godmanchester is '... *situated in the flat meadows which border that part of the Great Ouse, it is subject to a moist atmosphere of an unhealthy tendency, referred to by Mr. Philpot as the "malaria of Godmanchester "; but in its best days, the truth of God has flourished there, and particularly through the nineteenth century, when the Particular Baptist Church of which we wish to write was established and prospered,'* – so writes S. F. Paul in his opening words of description of the Baptist Chapel and Cause. [**S. F. Paul, 1958**: page 1] Given such a high accolade in its heyday, it is not difficult to appreciate the outward appeal the Chapel and group of Baptist Friends in the locality held for the Hercocks with their especially significant interest in the Cause and their commitment to it. The Baptist Chapel in East Street, originally built in 1796 (the year to which the Cause is known to date) and with its own burial ground within the curtilage of the property, was initially founded on Arminian doctrines (that is, as outlined by their promulgator, Jacob Arminius, in Holland) and continued in this mode until it was reformed on Particular Baptist principles broadly concurrently with the enlargement of the building in 1815. The change in style was occasioned by '... *a conflict within the Chapel community, which centred on a personal feud between Pastor Thomas Stevens Freeman and Mr. Edward Martin, the Squire of the town, who was a strong Arminian. This*

Godmanchester Particular Baptist Chapel

conflict was finally resolved after the Pastor had been exonerated of certain allegations made against him by the Squire.' [**S. F. Paul, 1958**: pages 2–5] In 1827 '... *a Sunday School was commenced in connection with the chapel, ... and in this way many of the children of the neighbourhood were brought under some orderly control on the Lord's day, and given a little instruction, which even in natural things was greatly wanting in those days.'* [**S. F. Paul, 1958**: page 12] A re–affirmation of the doctrinal basis of the Godmanchester Chapel was effected on Sunday, 31st July 1825, with a Declaration of Faith and Practice embodied in the Seventeen Articles of Faith (based on the 'Confession of Faith of the Particular Baptists'). The Chapel stood in ample grounds, fenced at the front (on the public thoroughfare) with attractive wrought iron railings; the decorative street–facing frontage of the building added its own element of sophistication to this magnificent–looking edifice.

Mr. Thomas Godwin, whom Henry Hercock had come to know so well and respect so highly during his time as Pastor at Potton, had commenced as Pastor at Godmanchester on the first Sunday in July 1861, and on 10th July he and his wife had moved into the Chapel House which stood in St. Ann's Lane. Mr. Godwin had been born at Purton (near Swindon), in Wiltshire, in 1803, the youngest son of a poor shoe–maker – so he and Henry Hercock had a real feeling for each other in the deep and full understanding of what their common, impoverished background had given (and denied) them. The people of the Baptist Cause at Godmanchester evidently took greatly to Thomas Godwin, as '... *there was much love and union between the people and their new Pastor. The Church increased in numbers, the new members being baptized in the River Ouse ... The cost of repairs and improvements to the Chapel and Chapel House ... was also freely met by the liberality of the friends. Mr. Godwin was then provided with a horse and carriage, for which a stable and coach–house were added to the Chapel House. Later on, a vestry for the minister was added to the Chapel, and also a Schoolroom which ... was opened ... on Aug. 18th 1868.'* [**S. F. Paul, 1958**: page 36] The Sunday–School room could accommodate up to two hundred children, giving a fairly graphic idea of the popularity of the Cause and Chapel in those days. Baptisms (of adult believers, not children, of course) used to take place in the River Ouse until 1879, but a Baptistry was built in the Chapel that year. When Mr. Godwin died in August 1877, he was one of the earliest Godmanchester Strict Baptists to be buried in the 'new burying ground' [**S. F. Paul, 1958**: pages 39 & 41] – which was within the grounds of the Parish Church of St. Mary the Virgin, Godmanchester, where, by agreement reached between the interested parties, an area of land within the bounding wall of the Churchyard had been set aside and designated for Nonconformist burials. Henry Hercock had travelled from Potton to be there, alongside many other Strict Baptist colleagues.

The Hercocks had established a great rapport with Mr. & Mrs. Godwin, had got to know Godmanchester Particular Baptist Chapel and its Friends well during the Potton years, and had retained these links from Leeds. Thomas Godwin and Henry Hercock had come to Supply each other's pulpits on numerous occasions during the 1870s – Henry was at Godmanchester Particular Baptist Chapel at least once in almost every year during that period, both during and after Thomas Godwin's life, and had continued to visit occasionally after his move to Leeds. [The Gospel Standard wrappers] Based on this evidence, it is likely the Hercock clan of the early 1890s had maintained their loose association with the Godmanchester Friends during their time at Biggleswade and Hitchin, so that when the unfortunate turn of events occasioned by the death of John Warburton at Biggleswade in 1892 prompted a rethink of their living arrangements, Godmanchester would immediately have been the place at the top of their list of possibilities. For, another favourite Pastor of theirs – in the person of Joseph Oldfield – who had been carving a notable reputation in Baptist circles, was now in post there.

After an interregnum of several years without a Pastor following Thomas Godwin, Mr. Oldfield had been invited to take the Pastorate of the Godmanchester Chapel in 1882. Initially he had declined the invitation, writing: *'To the Deacons and Members of the Particular Baptist Church meeting for the worship of the glorious Trinity in unity, in Cambridge Street, Godmanchester, – ... on the following day such a storm arose within my heart, that I feared we were all deceived together; for I had such a sight of my own unfitness, unworthiness, and poverty in spiritual things, that I felt of all upon the earth, the most unsuitable person to be a minister.'* [S. F. Paul, 1958: page 42] But, following a period of further, critical self–examination and mental anguish, finally he relented, and moved to the town where he soon won the hearts of his new flock. Well settled in this situation by the early years of the next decade, he and the Hercocks readily formed close bonds in their mutual allegiance to the Strict Baptist Cause at Godmanchester when the 'HERCOCK' family folk moved there and, in several seeking to become Members, presented their credentials before the Friends – little wonder, then, that Mr. Oldfield so gladly put their names forward to the Church Meetings. In giving to these Meetings their individual accounts '... of the Lord's dealings with their souls' (the typical phraseology entered in the **Church Book** records of such proceedings), members of the family would have given before the gatherings of the Friends their own candid testimonies of their past lives, including in each case an outline of an earlier life of existence in spiritual darkness, an exposition of how their conversion had come about leading them into the Baptist Cause, detailing events and moments of special blessings (including any apparently miraculous happenings) and spiritual elevation in the years that followed conversion, and so on. Such testimonies could be greatly moving and uplifting narratives to hear and be party to, frequently punctuated by such utterances from the audience as *'Praise be the Lord'* and *'Amen'*.

Thus it was this core group of the remaining family of Henry Hercock settled in geographical and – more significantly – spiritual terms for the foreseeable future, and proceeded to live their lives in the mould into which Henry had cast them by his conversion all those years before. Here in Godmanchester he lived on in them, as the 19th Century approached its close. Furthermore, Potton, just over 14 miles to the south, was easy to travel to by rail so that the 'HERCOCK' group over the border in Huntingdonshire was not far removed from their family's significant male personage, Charles James Hercock, his wife, Annie, and their children – the business here was thriving [Photograph: see page C3]. And, though separated by this small geographical distance, the members of these two groups all stood a coterie united in their common faith as well as sharing their deep feeling of being one family – which showed itself *inter alia* through their mutual respect for family values and honouring one another's persons, talents and abilities, similarities and differences. In short, Henry and his ethos was still their common bond, his spirit their enduring stream of life, his faith their characteristically impregnable strength.

A death around that time – indeed, in 1895 – though not then related in any manner with the 'HERCOCK' family, occurred at Sutton in the Isle of Ely, Cambridgeshire, when one Mary Markwell departed earthly life at approximately 60 years of age. Yet her passing was to impact on the 'HERCOCK' family just over a decade later, as destiny was to decree.

> Information about the death of Mary Markwell is from the later Obituary of William Markwell, her widower husband; and information about the couple's associations with the Sutton, Isle of Ely, Baptist Chapel is from Sutton Baptist Church records.

Sutton was just over fifteen miles from Godmanchester, lying roughly west of the great cathedral city of Ely which rises majestically above the low–lying, dark–soils of the Fens. This tight–knit, grittily misanthropic community was where William Markwell was a fenland farmer well–known locally as his family had been farming thereabouts for some generations. Both Mary and her husband, William, were stalwarts of the Sutton Baptist Chapel ('a *typical Nonconformist Meeting House, grey, square, plain, and substantial'* [**Ralph F. Chambers (unpublished manuscript), 1950s**]), in whose small burial ground Mary was probably interred. They had been Members since about 1888; and, showing in what respect and trust William was held by the Friends, he had been elected a Trustee the following year. It was his commitment to the Baptist faith that was to catalyse his later involvement with the Hercocks.

> The foregoing observation about the building at Sutton comes from an unpublished manuscript, from the 1950s, by Ralph F. Chambers (herein cited as '**Ralph F. Chambers (unpublished manuscript), 1950s**'), supplied to me by Mr. David J. Woodruff, Librarian of The Strict Baptist Historical Society, Dunstable, Bedfordshire.

❖ ❖ ❖ ❖ ❖ ❖ ❖ ❖ ❖ ❖ ❖ ❖ ❖ ❖ ❖ ❖ ❖ ❖

Into the Twentieth Century

Early Signs of Rough Waters Ahead

T he turn of the century – that symbolic marker of the passage of time on the calendar of human life and endeavour – brought with it new opportunities, fresh challenges and unforeseen trials. As with most other people of England, the Hercocks were to experience these phenomena just as did the rest; but added to their encounters of the common life of the country were some of their own, individual and highly personal ones. Perhaps the most tragic of the commonly–experienced events was the death of Queen Victoria on 22nd January 1901. The Hercocks will surely have been overtaken by the huge upwelling of emotion which was stirred by Victoria's demise, and will have shared in the nation's mourning. For it was truly the end of an era of huge importance in British history: she had reigned throughout a period embracing much of the Industrial Revolution, had been associated with the prodigious rise of the railways and of great steam ships; and she had restored the respect and dignity of Britain's monarchy which had been eroded by her predecessors. Overlapping the lives of Henry and Susannah Hercock, and their progeny, Victoria's reign had enormous influence over them all.

Beyond the Queen's passing, there were other great stirrings, for society in Britain was rapidly changing and the Edwardian era, now ushered in, was to expand and change the commercial and cultural life of the country beyond recognition. As the perceived hegemony of society at large over individual, personal conduct, which had characterised Victoria's reign, suddenly gave way to a burgeoning hedonism and carefree attitudes – particularly among the younger generations – a new and previously unforeseen fervour swept through Britain. Many of these changes were of a nature not to be highly favoured by the Hercocks, for the religious state of the nation was concurrently beginning to crumble, and a corrosive, slow mouldering of their Strict Baptist Cause was setting in – the remarkable influences and exceptional growth seen during its heyday in the 19th Century were not to return in their remaining earthly lifetimes. On a personal level, too, significant untoward developments were waiting in the wings.

It was the small family group of Josiah–John Hurlock and his wife Nellie Emily who were to be the very first in the wider 'HERCOCK' family to experience the personal pain of a death in their ranks when the infant Henry Ernest died on the very first day of the New Century – he was just 8 months old. It fell to his sorrowing mother to attend the Register Office at West Ham to register the event.

This sad happening aside, it was to be the Census of 1901, taken on 31st March, which was to provide the first official, comprehensive roundup of where the various family members were, and what they were doing, early in the new century.

Josiah–John, Nellie and their other children were still in Leyton, Walthamstow, where Josiah–John was recorded as 'Draper Dealer Shopkeeper', and employer working at home; the eldest daughter was recorded as 'Nellie'. Within the next few years the size of their family was to expand further, however, for Mrs. Hurlock's fecundity saw her producing another daughter, Laura, around 1902, and – in the autumn of 1903 – another son who took the forenames of his late deceased baby brother: Henry Ernest.

But Lucretia, Josiah–John's legitimate wife, had relocated yet again – this time to Wakefield, Yorkshire, where she was living with her younger son, Sydney, who gave his occupation as 'Secretary to Medical Man'. Lucretia now gave her marital status as 'widow'. Sydney's elder brother, John Henry, who had married in Wakefield Cathedral on 22nd June 1898, then naming and describing his father as 'Josiah Hurlock', a 'Traveller', was living with his wife, Ada, in a district of Hull; he worked as a 'Clerk and Book–Keeper'. As yet they had no children.

Also far flung, at 90 King Alfred Street, Derby, the widowed Lucy Ann Underwood, now 61 years of age, was living with her son, William Henry, who was still unmarried, but employed (as an Ironmonger's Assistant); they'd removed here from Nottingham in the latter part of the 1890s or, possibly, just before the time of Mr. Alfred Coughtrey's resignation from the Pastorate at Chaucer Street.

> There is scant evidence of the Underwoods' presence in Derby prior to the 1901 Census: Kelly's Directory of Derbyshire, 1899, lists two persons in Derby designated '*Underwood Mrs.*', giving no forename or initial, and neither of them lived at 90 King Alfred Street; however, Cook's Directory of Derby, 1900, lists William Underwood, an Ironmonger's Assistant, at 90 King Alfred Road *[sic]*. Wright's Directory of Nottingham, 1896–97, gives the currently last–known record of Lucy Ann Underwood there prior to her appearance in Derby, and various other sources (held at Nottingham Archives) of information about Nottingham residents fail to show her at any time later than this Wright's Directory entry. Thus, from this combined evidence, it would appear Lucy Ann and William Underwood left Nottingham during 1898 or 1899 and moved directly to Derby.

What the motivation had been to see them leave Nottingham after having been settled there for at least fifteen years is unknown, and their choice of Derby is rather enigmatic, too, as there does not appear to have been a particularly robust or alluring Baptist Chapel there at the time. The young William Henry's eldest sister (Eliza Jane), by contrast, was married: she and her husband, Harry Reginald Mumford, a Draper's Assistant, were living in Hackney, London, with a son and a daughter, both under the age of five. The youngest of the 'UNDERWOOD' clan, Helen Susannah (who'd been born around 1873 at Clipston, Northamptonshire), was also unmarried, working in Blackpool as a Fancy Leather Shop Assistant. The fragmentation evinced by this small family group was to typify circumstances in thousands of other families of this period as, increasingly, young people deserted their traditional family haunts in search of better–paid work in larger, or industrialised, cities, and to forge lives of different quality from those of their parents and earlier forebears.

The 'DUDDINGTON' group at Peterborough was, however, a remarkable exception to this family fragmentation, as Helen Letitia, her Carpenter husband, Joseph, and five of their younger offspring were at 'Olive House' where they had now lived since before 1881. One of the progeny still living at home was Ethel Eliza who had continued working as an Assistant in a Toy Shop, building on the experience she had begun a decade or so earlier when she'd lived in Biggleswade with her grandmother and Aunt Eliza Jane Hercock ... only now Ethel was working in her home city. Another of her sisters, Susie, was also working in the same line.

Ernie Hercock as a young man

As for all the others of the 'HERCOCK' family group, little had changed over recent years in their physical locations. At Potton, Charles James, Mary Annie and all but one of their offspring were to be found living in the same combined home–and– shop premises on the Market Square that 'CJ' had occupied for some thirty years. Bertram, their second son, was the only one who'd moved away by the time of this Census, to become an Apprentice to a Tailor and Hatter in Wellingborough. Charles Ernest, the eldest boy, still at home with his parents, had joined his father in the family business, working as a Printer's Compositor – a move which, though well intentioned on his father's part, was to prove futile as the teenager was already something of a wayward youth, difficult to manage and unruly in his general conduct. A considerable misfit among his siblings, Ernie (as he was known to them) was later to be labelled the 'black sheep' of his family. Ruth, the eldest girl, was now well advanced as a Pupil–Teacher at Potton's Board School, Edie was helping her parents out in the Shop and around house, and the younger offspring (Albert, Annie Christine and Wilfred Henry) were still school– children.

Then, up the road a few miles was the central 'HERCOCK' group, at Godmanchester. Henry's widow, Susannah, and their daughters, Eliza and Anna, were together occupying a house with more than five principal rooms. The Toy Shop in Post Street, of which Eliza was Proprietor, with Anna assisting, continued to give them a tolerably good income, and was operated from a large ground–floor room of the premises which fronted directly on to the public footpath running at the street's edge. The birth of a great–grandson to Susannah was soon to be the catalyst for the taking, during 1902, of a 'four–generations' photograph [Photograph: see page C5]; in it, the matriarch posed – in the award winning studio of A. Hendry at Godmanchester – with her daughter Helen Duddington, granddaughter Annie Stafford, and the latter's young baby boy, Leslie. This was a time when several of the family groups were availing themselves of the increasingly less costly art of studio photography to record their images for posterity.

Also in Post Street and just a short step away were Susanna Allen and her husband Thomas – he also continued in his Grocery business. The Baxters lived nearby, too, the Census confirming their presence, though they chose to show their business involvement only, stating the Huntingdon premises in George Street as their abode for the purpose of this exercise: William described himself as a 'Fancy Dealer (Shopkeeper)', whilst Mary Hayes gave her occupation as 'Fancy Bazaar'; both were employed on their 'Own Account', working from home – though they maintained a domestic residence in Godmanchester, as Kelly's Directory of 1903 was again to prove.

> Kelly's Directory of Huntingdonshire, 1903, lists *'Baxter William'* as a Private Resident; and, under the heading 'Commercial', lists *'Allen Thomas, shopkeeper'*, and *'Hercock Eliza Jane (Mrs.), toy repos'* – all in Godmanchester (the collated 'Trades' listing, at the back of this Directory, correctly lists under the heading 'Toy Dealers': *'Hercock Miss Eliza Jane, Godmanchester, Huntingdon'* – which confirms the *'Mrs.'* attribution in the local listing as an error). The same Directory lists at Huntingdon, under 'Commercial': *'Baxter William, fancy repository & china & glass warehouse, 3 George street'*.

Where were the three remaining orphaned offspring of William Henry and Mary Ann Hercock, and what were now their circumstances? Polly, yet single and In Service, had moved to St. Neots, Huntingdonshire, where she was a General Domestic Servant in the household of a retired pharmacist. So she was within ready travelling distance of her grandmother and aunts at Godmanchester and her uncle at Potton; and, though we have no record of any of them visiting each other, this would inevitably have happened from time to time. Walter, meanwhile, was working as a 'Plumber, Glazier, Gas and Hot Water Fitter' at Romford where he and Edie had already begun a family: their daughter, ordinarily known as 'Winnie', had been born there in February 1899. As for Fred, he was another who had made the subtle shift of surname spelling from 'HERCOCK' to 'HURLOCK' (there is also evidence he occasionally used 'HERLOCK'), and was living at West Ham, Essex, in the household of one Richard White (a Furniture Dealer) whose daughter, Florence Sarah Jane, he was to marry later in the year.

Of all these folk whom we have within our sights at this juncture, it was the apparently most long–settled, at Potton, who were to experience the next significant upheaval. In the aftermath of the damaging fire of January 1897, 'CJ' and Annie had been reappraising their circumstances and had taken a momentous decision about their future. However, initially biding their time to give their daughter, Ruth, an opportunity to complete her stint as Pupil–Teacher at the Board School, and to give some of their other offspring a chance to advance their education somewhat further, they had deferred for several years implementing the plan which they'd formulated. Their finances, so severely depleted by the outlay they'd had to make in recovering from the fire, weren't going to allow the couple to approach old age in the style they'd earlier hoped would be the case; and the business on the Market Square, though providing them with a more or less guaranteed, regular income, was so demanding on their time, not to mention their physical and mental resources, that they couldn't see how they were going to be able to persevere on this same tack for much longer – especially now that they'd had to use up so much of the 'fat' which had been put by previously for their intended eventual retirement. The plan they devised, then, was to move away and change their lives completely: 'CJ' would retrain as a Baker and they would hope to make a better living by this means in an environment where there was the potential for greater trade than Potton could provide. They therefore agreed to sell the business in Potton to Richard Elphick, a Printer colleague and Baptist friend from Biggleswade, and began making arrangements in the late summer and autumn of 1901 for the change–over which was to take place early in the new year. Ruth sat her Scholarship Examination for further Teacher Training that December, freeing the family to pack up and move on during January or February 1902 – by late February they'd gone, taking themselves and several of their offspring with them to their new surroundings in the east of London and Essex borders area. Far from bringing the middle–aged pair greater security and comfort, however, this drastic shift of both their work and location into hitherto unfamiliar areas heralded a period of enormously challenging precariousness, and unhappiness.

Times of uncertainty lay ahead also for the folk based in Godmanchester, where it cannot have been long after the start of 1901 that Thomas Allen first detected signs of a problem in his throat. This was diagnosed as cancer – it may be that Mr. Allen was a long–standing pipe–smoker. Watched in anguish by his wife and other family members, the disease progressed over the ensuing three years until the poor man died from it on 12th March 1904 (by which time he and his wife, Susanna, had moved from Post Street to a house in St. Ann's Lane, quite near the Chapel House). It was Thomas' granddaughter, Annie Louisa, one of the family with him at the end, who had the thankless task of presenting herself at the Register Office in Huntingdon three days later to provide an official record of her grandfather's death which had been certified by Herbert Lucas, M.R.C.S., of Huntingdon. The death certificate records Thomas Allen as a 75–year–old Master Grocer. Whilst there is no record in existence to show that he was buried at Godmanchester – it may be that he returned to Biggleswade, or even another place (such as Eaton Socon) where he had formerly lived, in order to find a final resting place – the Baptist Chapel's **Church Book** shows that he '*Died in the Lord*'. [**Godmanchester Strict Baptist Church Book, 1882– 1947**: Membership List, page 15] Thomas, knowing what was facing him, had had the foresight to ensure that his wishes would be carried out after his death, and to this end had prepared a Will in the autumn of the previous year; he appointed two of his friends as his Trustees and Executors (both attended the Godmanchester Particular Baptist Chapel). The Will was witnessed by his sisters–in–law, Eliza Jane and Anna Julia Hercock, who confirmed they were still spinsters. By this means Susanna, his widow, was to receive the rents of seven cottages which Thomas owned at Lower Caldecote in the Parish of Northill, Bedfordshire, for the remaining duration of her life, subject to her maintaining them in tenantable repair and insured; she was also to receive all her deceased husband's Personal Estate after payment of certain expenses and discharge of another bequest. Probate was granted at Peterborough on 11th April 1904 to one only of the Executors – Samuel Peacock, a Blacksmith of Huntingdon – the second Executor, Frederick William Brighty, a Commercial Traveller, of Godmanchester, having renounced the Probate (for an undisclosed reason). The Letters of Probate record that Thomas Allen had been a Retired Shopkeeper at the date of his death; his Estate was valued at £466 15s. 3d gross (equivalent to over £30,000 at today's values). It would seem that Susanna's income and financial security in widowhood were thus assured. Perhaps because the home she had shared in St. Ann's Lane with her husband was now too large and costly, Susanna moved some time after Thomas' death to another abode – in Godmanchester's London Street.

However, in the modern annals of the 'HERCOCK' family the greatest tragedy of the early years of the 20th Century was to be played out far away from rural Bedfordshire or Huntingdonshire, in the central area of the London conurbation.

◉ ◉ ◉ ◉ ◉ ◉ ◉ ◉ ◉ ◉ ◉ ◉ ◉ ◉ ◉ ◉ ◉ ◉ ◉

The Harringay Fire

If Thomas Allen's harrowing death caused great grief and hurt, what transpired in the lives of Josiah–John and Nellie Emily Hurlock and their children must have caused unimaginable shock. Living above the shop at 696 High Road, Leytonstone, by 1903 the couple had, apparently, had as many children as they intended, which was six. By this time Josiah–John was a Master Draper (that is he worked for himself as Proprietor of his own Drapery business) in Leytonstone where he had become something of a pillar of the community and was well known and liked. He was a Member of the charitable Salisbury Club, though he had lately resigned from the latter upon joining the City of London Mission in whose affairs he became an enthusiastic participant. But, around Christmas 1904 the family moved to different premises, at 393 Green Lanes, Harringay, London, where Josiah–John again ran his own Drapery shop and they all lived in rooms above it. It was here, in this bustling main thoroughfare running approximately in a north–easterly direction from near Regent's Park, through crowded parts of Camden, Islington and Stoke Newington, that a catastrophic incident was to take place one night in June 1905.

The **North Middlesex Chronicle** of Saturday, 1st July 1905 reported the happening most fully, as it was the newspaper serving the area in which the event occurred (what follows here is a facsimile transcription of the original):–

FATAL HARRINGAY FIRE.

TWO YOUNG LIVES LOST.

FATHER'S DESPERATE EFFORTS.

Harringay was early on Tuesday morn–ing the scene of a fire in which two young children lost their lives. The outbreak oc–curred at No. 393, Green–lanes shortly after midnight on Monday and in a very short space of time the premises in which a draper's business was carried on, was envel–oped in flames, and although every effort was made by the local fire brigades, two young children could not be got out of the building before they had succumbed to the smoke and flames. One of our reporters writes as fol–lows:–

Shortly after midnight on Monday evening a fire having fatal consequences occurred on the premises occupied by Mr. John Hurlock, draper, of Green–lanes, Harringay. A baker named Becker, whose premises adjoin those of Hurlock's, when going to his work noticed a light amongst some drapery in the shop. As it became brighter he concluded that the place was on fire. He thereupon battered at the door to arouse the inmates but failing in his purpose to wake them he went to the upper rooms in his own house and hammered at the side wall.

The premises were now well alight and an alarm was given to the Umfreville–street Fire Station of the Tottenham Fire Brigade. Im–mediately the firemen brought out their hy–drant, but at first the flames were so fierce that it was impossible to place the fire es–cape against the premises. The fire was gradually subdued and a fireman was enabled to enter the premises. On the second floor in the back part of the house he found the body of a girl. Other helpers had in the mean–time entered and they found a little child suffering agonising pains from several burns. She shortly afterwards died. The other members of the family escaped.

Several engines from Hornsey and Totten–ham arrived and their efforts prevented the fire from spreading, though the lower part of M. Hurlock's shop was entirely burnt out.

Mr. Hurlock, who was injured and had to be taken to the Tottenham hospital, has with his wife and six children occupied the premises since Christmas.

The Mother Tells Her Story.

The distracted mother tells the story of how the family found themselves when awakened from their sleep. She clutched her baby, a year and a half old, and the eldest girl took charge of the next youngest child. They were making their way down–stairs towards the flame and smoke, when the father, who had gathered the other children into the top back room, shouted " Come back ! Come back ! or you'll be suffocated!"

The mother turned and ran upstairs, call–ing after her, " Dorothy ! Dorothy !" to the eldest girl with the other child.

Pushing his wife, with the baby, out of the window, the husband secured their es–cape over a plank.

Three other children were got out the same way, and then the father, burnt and exhausted, fell from the window.

Dorothy, who had the remaining child, seems to have been overcome, for she was never seen again.

One of the boys, Fred, aged nine, also helped to remove the children and refused to leave the house until he was assured of their safety.

The two unfortunate children were after–wards removed to the Tottenham mortuary.

THE INQUEST.

The inquest on the bodies of the two children was held at Tottenham yesterday (Thursday).

Nelly Emily Hurlock, mother of the deceased children, said that, besides the deceased, there were four other children and her husband in the house at the time the fire broke out. There were no servants or assistants.

On Tuesday the shop was closed at ten o'clock at night, but witness remained there until a quarter to eleven. Witness had been in bed about a quarter of an hour when her husband came upstairs and about a quarter of an hour after that she heard her eldest girl knocking at the door and callin gout that people were

hammering at the front door and calling out
" Fire !" Witness was sleeping on the second
floor and the boys were on the first floor, Nel–
lie and Dora were sleeping in the same bed,
and Laura in a cot in the same room. Her
husband went down to the boys' room and just
afterwards shouted, " Upstairs, and get on to
the leads !" Her husband pushed witness out
on to the leads with the baby in her arms and
then Dora and the two boys got out. Witness
shouted, " Nellie, Nellie !" but no reply came
and she thought the poor child must have been
suffocated by then. Not more than five min–
utes had elapsed since the alarm was given.
When witness saw her daughter Nellie she had
the younger child in her arms.

Two men who came into the yard called to
witness to come down as she had the baby in
her arms, and witness replied, " I cannot.
There are two children in the house. " The
men said, " They will be rescued from the
front. " But witness could not go down until
planks were laid from the burning house to
the next house.

The jury returned a verdict that " Death was
due to suffocation from burns, " and added an
expression of sympathy with the relatives and
of their admiration of the way in which the fire
brigade and police had carried out their duties.

[North Middlesex Chronicle, Saturday, 1st July 1905]

The story first told by a local newspaper in Leytonstone was considerably less
detailed; here is the version printed by **The Leytonstone Express & Independent**
newspaper of the same date (what follows here is a facsimile transcription of the
original):–

THRILLING EXPERIENCE OF A FORMER LEYTONSTONE RESIDENT.

——— : o : ———

There were some thrilling scenes at a fire which
occurred in the early hours of Tuesday morning at
a draper's shop belonging to Mr. Hurlock in the
Green–lanes at Harringay. Miss Dorothy Hurlock
and her sister were suffocated, although there was
a fire station within fifty yards of the shop.

Residents in Leytonstone will remember that Mr. Hurlock formerly carried on a drapery business in the High–road. He was member of the Salisbury Club, which be resigned on joining the London City Mission, at Leytonstone, of which he became an enthusiastic member.

The firemen were at the shop within fifty seconds of the alarm being given, and it was not their fault that lives were lost. The fire broke out at one o'clock, and the occupants of the house were asleep. Next door is a shop kept by Mr. Becker, a baker, and his foreman was coming to make preparations for the morning baking. He noticed a light in Mr. Hurlock's shop and at once tried to rouse the in–mates. Miss Dorothy Hurlock, aged fourteen, was apparently awakened first. She roused her parents, and an attempt was made to escape by the back pre–mises.

In the meantime a hydrant had been got to work, and the flames in the shop were soon quelled. But the front of the premises was still full of smoke, and it was only possible to get out of the back windows, which the escape could not reach. Mr. Hurlock was seriously burnt in getting his wife and the younger children out.

It was discovered that the little girl, aged four, who was sleeping with Miss Dorothy Hurlock, was missing. Her sister, with the utmost bravery, ran back into the room, which was then full of dense and blinding smoke, to try and bring her out. But her efforts were in rain.

In attempting to save the life of her sister she sacrificed her own. Her deed of heroism was of no avail, for when the firemen got into the room they found her lying in the quiet sleep of death.

The other little girl was removed to Mr. Becker's, but she died in a few minutes.

[The Leytonstone Express & Independent, Saturday, 1st July 1905]

It will be noted that the two reports differ from each other in respect of several small points of detail and, in particular, over the forename of the older girl who died; the **North Middlesex Chronicle** gives her name as both 'Dorothy' and 'Nellie', whilst **The Leytonstone Express & Independent** gives it solely as 'Dorothy'. This information, which could have come from the girl's mother or a near–neighbour, suggests that the conflict over her forename which was apparent during the very first few weeks of the lass's life, had not, after all, been overcome; it could, therefore, have been the case that one parent wanted (and persisted in) calling her 'Dorothy' even though, to defer to the other parent (who insisted on 'Nellie'), the child's forename had been officially registered as the latter. All conflict on the issue was, however, put to rest when the unfortunate child's death was registered under the forename 'Nellie' just two days after the fire (following on more or less immediately from the Inquest which was held before Mr. A. M. M. Forbes, the Coroner for East Middlesex); since 'Nellie' is also used in that newspaper account portion which directly reports the words of the mother at the Inquest, it appears Nellie Emily had preferentially known her eldest daughter named 'Nellie'. The cause of death was certified as 'Shock from burns and suffocation from smoke, Accidental Causes'. It is presumed that the same cause of death was given officially for the other little girl, Laura (who was a toddler of about 3½ years).

The funerals of the two children had been held at Chingford Mount Municipal Cemetery, Essex, on Friday, 30th June, the remains of both having been interred in the same grave.

Page 2 of the following Saturday's edition of the **North Middlesex Chronicle** carried a short supplemental report recording the death of the children's father; published under the heading '*The Harringay Fatal Fire. – Another Death*', it reads:–

The death occurred at Tottenham Hospital on Monday morning, of John Hurlocke *[sic]*, who sustained severe burns in a fire which occurred at his drapery shop in Green–lanes, on Tuesday morning of the previous week. Deceased met with his injuries in his efforts to save his two children, Nellie and Laura, who were victims of the fire, the Inquest on whom we reported last week.

On the same day Josiah–John's death was similarly reported, though with a little more detail and with a reminder to readers that the deceased had been much esteemed locally, by **The Leytonstone Express & Independent** which proceeded to carry an open letter launching a public appeal to raise funds in support of the bereaved family. The letter, signed by three local men, commenced:–

The article in your valuable paper, re the sad calamity that has befallen Mr. Hurlock and family, has evoked widespread sympathy, and many have expressed a desire to show that sympathy in a tangible form ... we are sure you will be only too willing to open your columns for any subscription, however small, to help our former fellow citizens, who in addition to the loss of valuable young lives have also lost home and all they possessed. Word has just come that Mr. Hurlock has passed away, which makes the need all the greater.

Appended to this letter was a list of names of those who had already subscribed a total of £7 1s. 6d. (over £430 in today's money). By the end of the following week the appeal had raised a total of £24 9s. 6d. (over £1,500), with the addition of a further £8 14s. 6d. (over £535) by the end of the next week – bringing the grand total to some £33 4s. 0d. (over £2,000) by 22nd July when the appeal seems to have been closed and no further newspaper reports followed.

It had become apparent, as John Hurlock lay in his hospital bed, that he was going to die, so severe were his burns; accordingly, a Solicitor was called to his bedside to prepare a Will which John signed on 29th June. It must have been one of his last actions of any significance before he undertook the emotional farewells to his wife and children that would have preceded his last breath.

John Hurlock died on 3rd July in The Hospital on The Green at Tottenham, Middlesex, from 'shock from burns received on 27th June and Pneumonia supervening thereon, accidental causes', as recorded on his death certificate (which was issued on 5th July). A post–mortem had been carried out, but the Inquest held the day before the issue of the certificate sufficed for official purposes to ascertain what had befallen him, and how. His interment, on Wednesday, 5th July, was in the same grave as his two daughters at Chingford Mount Municipal Cemetery.

> Nellie, Laura and John Hurlock are buried together in Grave Number 69174 in Section D10 of Chingford Mount Municipal Cemetery; all three were 'Common Interments', and there is no memorial at the grave.

The Will (an official copy of which is transcribed here) is one of few tangible items from John Hurlock's life now still available.

THIS IS THE LAST WILL AND TESTAMENT of me JOHN HURLOCK of 393 Green Lanes Harringay in the county of Middlesex Draper I hereby revoke all wills and testaments by me at any time heretofore made and declare this to be my last will I give devise and bequeath unto my dear wife Nellie Emily Hurlock all my estate and effects whatsoever and wheresoever and whether real or personal for her own absolute use and benefit I appoint my said wife and my brother in law Alfred Mendham Rix of Waterlooville near Portsmouth Hampshire Ironmonger EXECUTRIX and EXECUTOR of this my will Dated this twenty ninth day of June one thousand nine hundred and five. John Hurlock. – Signed and declared by the said John Hurlock as and for his last will and testament in the presence of us both being present at the same time who at his request in his sight and presence and in the presence of each other have hereunto subscribed our names as witnesses – H LENTON LILLEY 287 High Road South Tottenham Solicitor – EMILY JANE LILLEY same address his wife.

On the 1st day of August 1905 Probate of this Will was granted to Nellie Emily Hurlock one of the Executors.

† †

Nellie Emily Hurlock and her children, circa 1909

At the time Probate was granted, the widowed Nellie Emily Hurlock and her surviving four children were living at 83 Cavendish Road, Green Lanes, Harringay – presumably temporarily with friends or in a Lodging House. The gross value of her deceased husband's Estate was £434 15s. 9d. (over £30,000 by today's values).

Some time later the surviving family of John Hurlock was to leave the London area to settle in Waterlooville, Hampshire, near Nellie Emily's brother. Behind them they would leave an ordeal from which it must have taken years to recover. Their memories of the brave man who had sacrificed his life to do as much as he could to save his family must have been forever marred by the shockingly vivid final images from the night of the fire – and the days thereafter when the poor man lay dying in hospital and the survivors had to bury three of their most loved ones. In Waterlooville Nellie Emily eventually opened a Millinery shop; Dora lived at home with her mother until, eventually, she married (though was to remain childless), but the three boys had been despatched elsewhere – and somewhat paradoxically – Victor to a Home for Homeless Boys, and both Fred and Henry Ernest to a boarding school for orphans.

Dora May Hurlock on her
wedding day, 1928

The question of who John Hurlock really was, and the story of how I discovered what had happened in the life of Josiah Hercock or Hurlock, appears in detail in **Appendix One**: '*Who was John Hurlock?*'.

1911 Census:–

Nellie Emily Hurlock, widow aged 43 years, a Draper (Proprietor), and Dora May Hurlock, aged 16 years, a Pupil Teacher in the employ of the County Council, both living at Sydney Villa, Waterlooville, Hampshire.

Victor Hurlock, aged 13 years, living in the 'Home for Little Boys' (a Home for Homeless Boys) at South Darenth, Dartford, Kent.

John F. Hurlock, aged 15 years, and Henry E. Hurlock, aged 7 years, both living in one of the 'Warehousemen, Clerks' and Drapers' Schools (an Orphan School) at Purley, Surrey.

⊚ ⊚ ⊚ ⊚ ⊚ ⊚ ⊚ ⊚ ⊚ ⊚ ⊚ ⊚ ⊚ ⊚ ⊚ ⊚ ⊚ ⊚ ⊚ ⊚

Diminishing Numbers

Gradually, news of the tragedy which had unfolded at Harringay reached Josiah's blood relations. First to hear was probably his emotionally–nearest sister Helen Letitia Duddington in Peterborough, or his elder brother Charles James Hercock. Quite how the news got out, and to whom initially, we shall probably never know, but that Josiah had maintained some sort of contact with one or both of these two of his siblings is proven by the fact that a postcard which had been sent to him about this time, but clearly never received by him, found its way eventually to 'CJ'.

This postcard – showing an atmospheric picture of Potton Market Place, including the shop and home premises which had once been the preserve of William Henry Hercock and, latterly, of Charles James Hercock – was posted from Potton in the late afternoon of 1st July 1905, addressed to 'Mr. Herlock'. Although the message written on the postcard suggested it could, apparently, have been relevant either to Josiah or to 'CJ', it was to be proved many years later that Josiah had been the intended recipient, but that 'CJ' had ended up with it as his younger brother had died before the postcard could be delivered to him.

Just what 'CJ' and the wider 'HERCOCK' family made of the news of Josiah's death and the catastrophe that had befallen his bigamous wife and children, we shall probably never know for it seems that no–one kept a diary or wrote down any thoughts about, or reactions to, the event. That Josiah had made a bigamous marriage and disguised the fact by taking an alias would surely have caused many of his siblings to distance themselves from him for, in their own deepest faith and commitment to the Christian – and, more significantly – Baptist way of life, the likes of Mary Hayes Baxter, Eliza Jane Hercock, Susanna Allen and 'CJ' could never have accepted this as an honest or

Potton Market Square in the early twentieth century
[The shop formerly run by William Henry Hercock, and run up to early 1902 by Charles James Hercock, is the white–fronted building centre–right, behind the line of children]

honourable course for their younger brother to have taken. They would doubtlessly have seen Josiah's legitimate widow, Lucretia, and children as the principal victims of the piece; and, although hearts may have softened towards Nellie Emily and her children in their painful loss of the most significant man in their lives, and all their possessions, it's highly improbable that any of them would ever have been received as members of the wider 'HERCOCK' family. Certainly, there was no known documented meeting, or written exchange, between any of them and any of the other 'HERCOCK' family. Nor, as it happens, was there any known documented meeting, or written exchange, between Lucretia (or any of Josiah's blood relations descended from her) with her erstwhile husband's siblings or others. The absence of documented meetings or written exchanges is not, of course, conclusive evidence of what, if any, contacts there were. However, it seems likely that both of Josiah's widows and their respective children were henceforth left to pursue courses through life which kept them separate from most of their 'HERCOCK' relations, a situation which arose principally through Josiah having cut himself off from his parents and siblings.

It is not surprising, then, that following the immediate aftermath of the tragedy at Harringay, the majority of the wider 'HERCOCK' family members generally put memories of their unwanted and/or unknown relations – who had arisen from the maverick Josiah, the one sibling who had never seen eye–to–eye with his 'HERCOCK' sisters and brothers – to the backs of their minds, and proceeded to get on with their own lives. Some of them, too, were having to grapple with their own demanding and stressful difficulties.

◉ ◉ ◉ ◉ ◉ ◉ ◉ ◉ ◉ ◉ ◉ ◉ ◉ ◉ ◉ ◉ ◉ ◉ ◉

Unsettled Times

For some years after leaving Potton, life for 'CJ' and Mary Annie was unsettled, with 'CJ' changing jobs often – working at times in the bakery trade and at other times in the printing trade (perhaps to help bring in a better weekly wage when bakery work was hard to come by) – and Annie suffering ill health, probably provoked by the unrelenting stresses of their working and living circumstances. Among the many places they lived were Maldon, Essex, and Romford – in the latter, they lived awhile in Palm Road which is where Walter, Edie and their young children were also based (their other nephew, Fred, now married and with a young son, Richard Walter, was also not far from there). It was while they were at Maldon that Ruth finally gained her Teaching Certificate, after successfully passing the Cambridge External Examination, and began teaching at a local elementary school. In Maldon, where she remained after her parents had moved on again, Ruth met Richard Robert William Flowerday (known as 'Will'), an Apprentice to a local Ironmonger, and the two of them became close friends, sharing attendances at Maldon Baptist Chapel in Crown Lane. Will Flowerday, who originated from the East–Norfolk village of Ingham where he'd been christened (in 1883) in a Primitive Methodist Chapel of the North Walsham Circuit, was now living in

Walter, Edie and their children at Romford

lodgings at Maldon, while Ruth was in a hostel for young unmarrieds. They became engaged during 1907; Will, converted to the Baptist faith, underwent Believer's Baptism in the Maldon Baptist Chapel during June of that same year, and Ruth did likewise the following year – though not until after their marriage. [From the **Membership Book of Maldon Baptist Church**]

Before that happy occasion could take place, though, the wider family was again emotionally rocked ... this time by the death of the matriarch, Susannah Hercock, Henry's widow, at Godmanchester. At almost 94 years of age, Senile Decay had finally caught up with the once–stalwart lady in her home at Post Street. Even though the general deterioration in her physical condition had been progressing for several years, her mental faculties had remained quite sharp; her demise, when it came, was an enormous shock to her loved ones. Surrounded by many members of her closest family as she breathed her last, Susannah slipped peacefully away. Her passing marked the end of an era and, for her offspring, the shattering of the last tangible link with their late father. It fell to her step–granddaughter, Annie Louisa Allen, to walk to nearby Huntingdon two days later to register the old lady's death, the date of which was recorded on the death certificate as 23rd March 1907.

Susannah's mortal remains were interred (on 27th March) in a grave in the Churchyard of the Parish Church of St. Mary the Virgin, in that part of the Churchyard which had been set aside for Nonconformist burials.

> The date of death on the death certificate is erroneous, as both the Obituary and the local newspaper's announcement show. As death occurred after midnight, it was not on Saturday, 23rd March, but rather Sunday, 24th March, on which Susannah's death apparently took place.

THE FRUITS OF HIS LABOURS

> The date of the interment comes from records of burials in the Nonconformist Burial Ground in the Parish Churchyard of St. Mary the Virgin, Godmanchester, now held by the authorities of the Parish Church. The grave plot had been purchased by a 'Miss Hercock' – who would have been none other than Eliza Jane.

Attended by her several daughters and her son 'CJ', as well as spouses and various of their offspring, and by Baptist friends and others from the locality, Susannah's moving funeral service in the Godmanchester Baptist Chapel was officiated by her friend, Pastor Joseph Oldfield, who went on to pen an Obituary of her which was published in **The Gospel Standard**. This is what he wrote (here is an accurate transcription from the original):–

SUSANNAH HERCOCK, of Godmanchester, widow of Henry Hercock, minister of the gospel, departed this life peacefully in the Lord on March 24th, 1907, in the 94th year of her age.

Our beloved sister in the Lord was called by grace when about 19 years of age. She had a very blessed deliverance from the powers of darkness, and translation into the kingdom of God's dear Son. She was baptised by Mr. Tiptaft in the Factory chapel at Oakham, in the year 1844, and joined the church there under the pastorate of Mr. Philpot. She had a large family, and was much tried in providence, which caused her at times to question the reality of her former deliverance, and her interest in the love of God. Once it was much laid on her mind, " If thou faint in the day of adversity, thy strength is small ; " and from that she knew a time of adversity was at hand. Directly after, the Russian war began, which proved the greatest time of temporal trial and adversity she and her husband ever experienced. She was often in a very exercised state, fearing after all she should be deceived. Of late years she has been much looking forward to what the end would be, so often she would say, " How will it be with me then ? "

About two years ago she had a very special time in the night. The words were applied to her, " Take, eat ; this is My body ; " which were both meat and drink to her for many days. Satan frequently assailed and tried to rob her, but she used to say he could not rob her of this. Many times after Satan's assaults the Lord has given her some precious word or line of a hymn, by which she has been victorious over the enemy. Nearly every morning she has spoken of some word she has had to comfort her. Once she had very specially the lines :

> " The Saviour, whom I then shall see
> With new, admiring eyes,
> Already has prepared for me
> A mansion in the skies."

A few months before her end this verse was much on her mind –

> " Lord, let Thy sacred love employ
> My musings all day long ;
> Till in the realms of purest joy
> I make it all my song."

The last time Satan was permitted to assault her was on March 19th. She said to her daughter, " I have had a sad night. For a time all my religion seemed wrong ; I thought I was quite deceived. Satan is a great enemy ; but it is better now. I know I am right, and waiting God's time to take me home." About two years ago her sight failed her, so that she could not read, which was a great trial to her.

In the afternoon before her departure I saw her and read part of John xiv., and engaged in prayer, to which she responded suitably. She was so calm and peaceful that the thought of death so near could hardly enter into one's mind. During the night she repeated correctly the *whole* of the hymn commencing,

" Jesus, Lover of my soul."

At midnight she exclaimed, " Just outside the gate," and shortly afterwards " Hallelujah ! " and then immediately her ransomed spirit took its flight to her eternal home with Christ in glory. Devout men carried her mortal body to her burial, which was in sure and certain hope of the resurrection unto eternal life, through Jesus Christ our Lord.

J. OLDFIELD.

[**The Gospel Standard**, 1907: pages 279–281]

◎ ◎ ◎ ◎ ◎ ◎ ◎ ◎ ◎ ◎ ◎ ◎ ◎ ◎ ◎ ◎ ◎ ◎ ◎

The local newspaper, **The Huntingdonshire Post**, carried the following announcement on the Saturday following Susannah's death:–

GODMANCHESTER   Nonagenarian's Death.–Shortly after mid–night on Saturday the oldest lady resident in the Borough in the person of Mrs. Susannah Hercock, widow of Rev. Henry Hercock passed away at the advanced age of 94. Mrs. Hercock was a Miss Hayes and a native of Langham, Rutlandshire, where she married Mr. Hercock who was a Baptist Minister, and held pastorates at Leeds *[sic]*, Potton (Beds.) and Peterborough.

Some time later the family arranged for the erection of a magnificent headstone at her grave on which was inscribed:–

In Loving Memory of Susannah, Widow of Henry Hercock (Baptist Minister), who died March 24ᵗʰ 1907 Aged 93 years. 'So he giveth his beloved sleep. Ps. 127. 2.'

> I first visited the Parish Churchyard of St. Mary the Virgin, Godmanchester, and discovered my great–great–grandmother's last resting place, on 13ᵗʰ June 2002. In the peace of the Churchyard, the grave is beneath the canopy of several large, leafy trees – an admirably suitable place for the worldly–wearied to spend their final sleep, awaiting the day of The Resurrection. The grave was originally delineated by a surrounding stone kerb, but there is no longer any sign of that; the headstone is still in excellent condition now (2011). [Photograph: see page C1]

The Reverend Henry Hercock's widow, the ever–loyal and devoted Susannah, survived him by some twenty–six years. She had been Henry's indomitable support and loyal companion throughout his life's work, then, after his passing she had carried his spirit ever onward through the way she lived in widowhood. Undeniably, there was ample justification for the people to whom her husband

The artistry of Susannah Hercock's grave memorial

had ministered to extend their appreciation to her for her untiring, unwavering, contribution. Susannah's death must have once more created a deep, dark void in family circles, and her daughters in Godmanchester will have been particularly wounded to the core by her loss.

Naturally, friends at Chapel will have shared in the period of mourning which followed, but, despite this, continuity of normal life had to be preserved as ably as possible, and this applied both to the individuals of Henry and Susannah's family as well as to the groups of extra-family folk with which they were associated, yet who were touched by Susannah's recent death. Thus, at a meeting of the Trustees and Members of the Particular Baptist Chapel in Godmanchester, which had been called for Wednesday, 16th October 1907 (and which continued by adjournment on 6th November), it is not surprising to find that Mary Hayes and William Baxter, as well as Eliza Jane Hercock, were present along with some forty–two other Members, the serving Trustees, and the Minister, Reverend Joseph Oldfield (who took the Chair). The business of the meeting being that important task of appointing new Trustees to replace several who had died, the 'HERCOCK' family folk will have exercised due deliberation in their choice of persons to be elevated to these responsible positions within the local Baptist community. [**Godmanchester Strict Baptist Church Book, 1882– 1947**: page 104]

It was in this very year of 1907 that William Markwell's destiny became inextricably linked with the Hercocks. For it was then that the widower of some twelve years, still living at Sutton in the Isle of Ely, cemented his relationship with Susanna Allen. Introduced through their mutual Baptist connections, they had come to know each other in the course of practising their common faith and their Chapel involvements; their friendship was to grow to the point where, eventually, William proposed to Susanna whom he now took as his second wife. Their marriage that September was held in the Register Office at Ely, where the two witnesses to the signing of the Register were Robert Thompson Senescall and his wife Ida Mary, née Markwell (a sister of William). Her remarriage at the age of 63 years was to bring back to Susanna's life a measure of male company which she'd missed since the death of her first husband, but the cost was that she now was to move from her modestly comfortable home in London Street and the closeness she enjoyed with her sisters, to the relatively austere surroundings of a farmer's abode in the small, isolated fenland village of Sutton which completely lacked the charms and amenities of Godmanchester and Huntingdon. Quite what Susanna's siblings made of this match would have been interesting to know! Fortunately, Sutton being sufficiently close to Godmanchester for mutual visits to have been relatively easy to undertake, Susanna could still see her blood relations when she wished. Moreover, as it appears she retained her Membership at the Baptist Chapel in Godmanchester [**Godmanchester Strict Baptist Church Book, 1882–1947**: Membership List, page 15 – in this List, Susanna Allen's surname had been altered to 'Markwell', further evidence of her continuation here], it is presumed Susanna would have made her way there on a fairly regular basis to attend Communion and other services. Bravely acknowledging her changed marital status, Susanna now added her new name, 'S Markwell', to the inscription in the front of her personal copy of her late father's ***Memoir***, without, however, striking out the earlier inscription which named both herself and her erstwhile husband, Thomas Allen – such was the esteem in which she evidently held his memory.

At the time of this marriage neither of the parties would have had in mind the possibility of death – quite the opposite, one supposes. Yet, it is thoughts of death that tend to come to the forefront of the minds of ageing folk – or those who are seriously ill. As she was barely into her fifties, this latter reason may have been the case with Lucretia, Josiah's first wife, who was living in Upper Tooting, London, when she decided to have her Will drawn up, and signed it on 24th December 1906. Perhaps this was merely a precaution, fearing death was not far off. However, whatever the reason, she was to be fortunate to be spared to live on a good many years beyond this, though she was virtually destitute, living in greatly impoverished circumstances. She may have been dependent on the generosity of her younger son, Sydney, who lived with her; John Henry, the older son, was then living at Hessle, near Hull, Yorkshire. Whether Lucretia was visiting friends in Nottingham at the time, or whether the friends had travelled to London to see her, we don't know – but the two witnesses to her signing of the Will were a mother and daughter who gave a Nottingham address.

Illness and failing health were evident in other areas of the family, too. In the depths of the winter of 1908, Anna Julia Hercock, still living at Godmanchester with her elder sister, Eliza (who, incidentally, had continued to run her Toy–Shop from their home), died on 4th February, after having contracted Pneumonia a week earlier. She was 65 years old, and had until almost the end continued to work as an Assistant in her sister's Shop. It was not her sister, Eliza Jane, however, who took upon herself the task of attending the Register Office at Huntingdon to register the death; rather, it was Anna's younger sister, Helen, who had come from Peterborough to be with Anna at her ending, sitting with the bedridden spinster – with whom she had had a friendly, warm relationship through adult life – right to the very moment of death. Helen undertook the short walk to Huntingdon to discharge this duty on that very same day – soon after Anna had passed away, perhaps as a means of getting a breath of fresh air to help her over the initial shock and utterly piercing grief of those first few minutes and hours immediately after experiencing at such close quarters the death of a loved one.

> Kelly's Directory of Huntingdonshire, 1906, under the heading 'Commercial': 'Hercock Eliza Jane (Mrs.), [sic] toy repos[itory], Godmanchester'; also in the aggregated Trades Directory, under 'Toy Dealers': 'Hercock Miss [sic] Eliza Jane, Godmanchester, Huntingdonshire'.

The following Saturday's newspaper printed the following short report:–

GODMANCHESTER We regret to record the death of Miss Anna Julia Hercock, fourth daughter of the late Pastor Hercock, which took place after a very short illness at her residence in Post–street on Tuesday, at the age of 65.
[**The Huntingdonshire Post**, Saturday, 8th February 1908: page 8, column 4]

... and this separate announcement appeared in the Births, Marriages, and Deaths column:–

DEATHS. Godmanchester, Feb. 4, Anna Julia Hercock, 65.
[**The Huntingdonshire Post**, Saturday, 8th February 1908: page 8, column 8]

The date of her funeral is not known, nor are many other details, but Anna was interred in the Nonconformist section of the Parish Churchyard of St. Mary the Virgin, near her mother's grave. The inscription on her gravestone reads:–

In Loving Memory of Anna Julia, fourth daughter of the late Henry & Susannah Hercock, who died Feb 4th 1908. Aged 65 years. 'And a book of remembrance was written before him for them that feared the Lord, and that thought upon his name.' mal. 3. 16

> I discovered Anna Julia Hercock's grave during my first visit to the Parish Churchyard of St. Mary the Virgin, Godmanchester, on 13th June 2002. The headstone is in fair condition now (2011). [Photograph: see page C6]

Not endowed, in the grand scheme of things when the distribution of brains and vitality was being made, with great intelligence or intellect, Anna Julia was, by nature, something of a dullard. Willing enough to do as she was asked or told, provided she was given sufficient instruction or a demonstration of what was required, she would undertake other people's bidding whether the task was mindlessly mundane or repulsively vile, but seldom, if ever, could or would she act on initiative. She was a follower rather than a leader; harmless enough, she meant well, but achieved little of note on her own account; yet, she had been a dutiful, attentive daughter and sister. Throughout her life she'd been part of the family furniture, utterly dependent on her parents and siblings for financial and emotional support and benignly accepted by them as she frequently traversed from one home to the other so as not unduly to burden any one. Eventually, though, as we've seen, it was her next elder sister, Eliza, who took Anna more or less permanently under her wing and, conveniently, was able to make use of her limited abilities in assisting with simple tasks around the Toy–Shop. In this it appears Anna was, finally, content and also, living under the same roof as their increasingly frail mother, gave the latter what care was needed until the old lady's demise just the year before Anna herself. In this latter rôle, then, Anna had performed valuable and appreciated service not only to her mother, but also to her siblings in relieving them of much of that particular burden. If anything penetrated to her emotional core sufficiently to wound it beyond repair, it must surely have been the death of her dear mother – and that was probably the main cause of Anna's demise so soon after.

Perhaps prompted in some measure by his mother's death – an event which will have concentrated their minds on preserving their own well–being – 'CJ' and Annie had to rethink, once again, their strategy for life as the nomadic existence they were living before 1908 was taking its toll on them, with Annie's health failing seriously. 'CJ' had, by then, made sufficient progress in learning the bakery trade for them to risk setting themselves up in that line of work; the next requirement, then, was to decide where to base themselves. They missed the provincial rural environment to which they'd grown accustomed during so many years in Potton, that it seemed the most logical thing to return to that sort of locality. It was, of course, out of the question that they should return to Potton itself; rather, they needed a somewhat larger community from which they could draw sufficient trade and an income adequate to enable them to build up their monetary reserves once more. Thus, when an opportunity arose to rent from a local resident a Tea–Room and Bakery in Church Street, Dunstable – one of the burgeoning and rapidly prospering south Bedfordshire towns of the early 1900s – they plumped for it, moving in during the early months of 1908.

The first official sighting we have of 'CJ' and family at this precise location comes from the Inland Revenue's Land Values Duty records dating from 1910: in the Register, Charles James Hercock is recorded under Assessment No. 2293 as Occupier of a House & Shop in Church Street, and under Assessment No. 2294 as Occupier of a Building in Church Street, both owned by Hannah Emma Derbyshire (who resided at 1 Victoria Street, Dunstable); the Map accompanying the Register, based on the earlier (1901) Ordnance Survey map of Dunstable, shows the property marked with Assessment No. 2293 as being at the very top (west end) of Church Street adjacent the junction with the High Street, and on the south side of Church Street, commensurate with the location at Number 1 Church Street which is known to have been the full address (there is no property marked with Assessment No. 2294, but a small out–building in a yard behind the House & Shop of Assessment No. 2293 is probably what was encompassed in Assessment No. 2294).

Charles James Hercock and his wife
Mary Anne, née Baxter

Scarcely had the dust settled from 'CJ' and Annie's move to the town, than the wedding of Ruth Hercock and Will Flowerday took place in Dunstable's West Street Particular Baptist Chapel. It was the first most felicitous event of 'CJ's and Annie's newest phase of life to have happened – on Wednesday, 17th June 1908. The celebration of this wedding (the first of the couple's offsprings' marriages) facilitated the greatest ever photographically–recorded gathering together of members of the extended 'HERCOCK' family – yet, understandably, the event will have been tinged with sadness at the very recent passing of close members of the family, particularly 'CJ's sister, Anna, and their mother, Susannah. Inevitably, thoughts will have wandered to the tragic irony that the 'HERCOCK' matriarch should have been denied the pleasure of attending such a grand occasion as this special family wedding, and that the bride should have had to forego her grandmother's presence on her otherwise happy day.

Ruth was blessed that day with the presence of all but one of her siblings, and it was her nearest sister, Edie, who attended her as adult Bridesmaid. There also were several 'BAXTER' cousins and others from the Peterborough area. The eldest and most venerated of family members attending was Ruth's Aunt Mary: Mary Hayes Baxter, who had travelled from Godmanchester. A short, wiry, lady with a broad forehead and a face now tapering sharply to the chin, she was on the threshold of her seventieth birthday. The rather severe expression on her face that day, as she stood behind and slightly to the left of her scowling nephew, Charles Ernest Hercock, for the large group photograph, belied the gentle manner which lay beneath. 'Great Aunt Mary' (as she was affectionately known amongst younger generations of the family) was turned out entirely in black, probably to signify her continuing state of mourning for recently–deceased loved ones; with one or two exceptions, all other ladies present were in white. Although the attribute of being the youngest there was not

Edith Hercock as a young woman

Wilfred Henry Hercock's, he was, even so, the bride's youngest sibling, who sat – legs crossed – at her feet; but, standing to Ruth's left, 9½–year–old Winnie Hercock from Romford ranked at the very opposite end of the age scale from Great Aunt Mary, and was the second Bridesmaid. And, although young Winnie's parents (Walter and Edie) weren't present, her father's elder sister – first cousin of the bride – was. She, of course, was Polly Hercock, herself yet unmarried, who had not long crossed the threshold of her forties. [Photograph: see page C7]

Polly, or Mary Ann Sawyer Hercock (to give her her full name) – the only daughter of the erstwhile founder of **The Potton Journal** (the organ that had been his downfall in all conceivable senses), the ill–fated William Henry Hercock – whose experience of having been cruelly created an orphan on the death of her

Great Aunt Mary and Polly on Ruth Hercock's wedding day

Grave memorial at Brauntson–in–Rutland of Henry Hercock's sister, Mary Springthorpe, and her husband

Susannah Hercock's grave memorial at Godmanchester

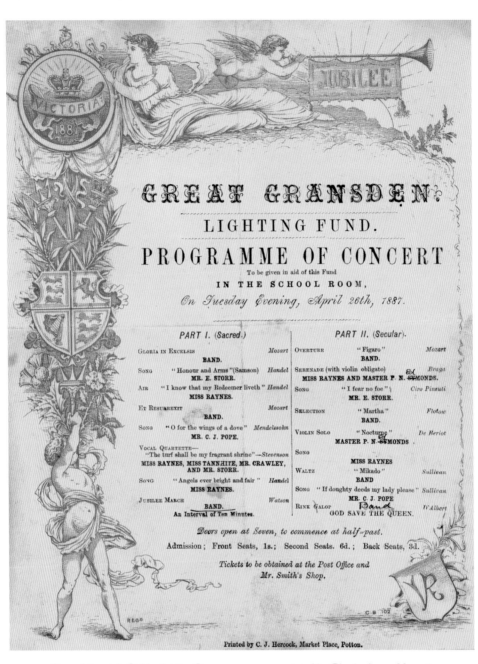

Queen Victoria's Golden Jubilee Concert programme printed by Charles James Hercock

Market Place, Potton, Beds., Midsum 1895

Mr. A. Sinn

Bought of C. J. HERCOCK,
PRINTER, BOOKBINDER,
WOOL, TOY, HABERDASHERY, STATIONER, AND FANCY REPOSITORY, BOOKSELLER,
Paperhanger, Newsvender.

Departments.	1895		£	s.	d.
Printing. Letterpress Printing of all kinds. Bills Circulars, Cards, Billheads, Pamphlets etc.	Jan. 2	3 Account Books		2	0
	12	Paste 6 Blotting Paper 9		1	3
Stationery. Black and Coloured Inks. Note Paper from 4½d. per 5-quire packet. Envelopes from 1½d. per packet. Black-bordered and Fancy Paper and Envelopes. Blotting Paper, Tissue Paper, plain and cut out. Embossed Dish Papers. Curling Papers. Account Books from 1d. Slates and Pencils. Pens and Penholders. Birthday Cards and Books. Sixpenny and One Shilling Boxes of Plain and Fancy Note Paper and Envelopes.	21	Labels 6 Ink 4 Pocket Book 6		2	0
		250 White Envelopes printed		2	6
		100 large memos.		3	0
		200 small "		3	0
Bookselling. A heavy stock of Cloth Bound Books, from 4d. each. Bibles, Hymns, Prayers, Prayers and Hymns, etc.	Feb.	1,000 tinted Envelopes, print		12	
		120 Circulars 3/1 100 Post Cards		10	0
Haberdashery. Berlin Wool, single and double, Scotch Yarn. Petticoat Wool. Fleecy, Beehive Shetland, Andalusian and a large variety of other Fancy Wools. Crochet and Sewing Cotton, Knitting Pins Crochet Hooks, Needles and Pins, Pearsall's Knitting and Crewel Silks, Filoselle, Antimacassars and other work. Mendings. Knitting Cottons.	Mar.	250 white Envelopes		2	6
		400 memos. 2 ups		7	6
	20	600 Billheads 3 "		7	6
	Apl.	3 Books 3/1 ½ letters		3	0
	30	500 small memos		7	0
Toys. Drawing Slates, Dominoes, Draughts and Boards, Hoops, Wheelbarrows, Trains, Scales and Weights, Horses and Carts, Tea Sets, Dolls, Perambulators, Engines, Drums, Skipping Ropes, Balls, Marbles, Tops, A large stock of tin toys, Rattles, Hammers, Mallets, Watches, Horns, Tin Whistles, Whips, Guns, Traps and Balls, Pails, Puzzle Blocks, Spades, Noah's Arks, And a large stock of other goods too numerous to mention. Swiss Bricks. Nine Pins. Leather Reins. Fishing Tackle, Cricketing Materials.		Note Paper 9 A/c Book 4		1	9
	May 1	250 white Envelopes		2	6
		300 large memos		6	0
	" 20	Note Paper 9 Order Book 6		1	3
Fancy Goods. Ink Stands various kinds, Writing Cases and Desks, Work Boxes, Albums, Ladies Companions, Needles Cases, Blotters, Papeteries, Watch Stands, Letter Racks, etc. Photograph Frames, Work Baskets, lined and unlined, Pencil Cases, Plush Pouches, Pen and Pocket Knives, Ladies and Gents Bags, Fancy China, Purses, Pocket Books. Glove and Handkerchief boxes, Money and other Boxes, Birthday Text Books, Christmas and Birthday Cards, Papier machie Trays, and other articles. Large stock of Ladies Bags.	Jun 19	200 Small Cards			9
		Printing 110 Post Cards 2 ups		7	0
		Settled	£ 4	2	0

With thanks

A. Hercock

Fob watch in a satin–lined case inscribed with Willy Hercock's name and other details

Susannah Hercock in a 4-generations photograph, 1902

Anna Julia Hercock's grave
memorial at Godmanchester

Eliza Jane Hercock's grave
memorial at Godmanchester

Wedding photograph of
Richard Robert William Flowerday and Ruth Hercock, 1908

Memorial Plaque: Eddie Bowen

A surviving relic of the former Particular Baptist Chapel, Godmanchester

mother some thirty years earlier and of having been confined in the Orphanage had helped mould her personality, had turned out another gentle lady, soft in manner and understanding and loving at heart. She had been living for some while with her Aunt Eliza Jane at Godmanchester – probably helping out in the Toy–Shop – and was now engaged to marry a bachelor some twenty years her senior. There can be little doubt she will have been picking up a few ideas and tips at the wedding of her cousin, where Polly – a buxom lady smiling benignly for the photograph – stood next to her Uncle James Baxter, near the opposite end of the group from Great Aunt Mary and, like the latter, also fully dressed in black.

So it came about that Polly herself walked down the aisle – of the Godmanchester Baptist Chapel – on Tuesday, 22nd September 1908 when she wed, *'According to the Rites and Ceremonies of the Particular Baptists'*, George Ambrose. Her husband also lived in Post Street and took paid Gardening work locally to earn a crust. Polly's Aunt Eliza was, perhaps, the most natural choice of witness to the signing of the Register at the ceremony at which the Pastor, Joseph Oldfield, officiated, whilst Walter Charles Sawyer – Polly's cousin from Peterborough – was the second witness.

Was this, however, a truly happy occasion? Apart from the slight disappointment and annoyance that the local newspaper made something of a mess of the announcement of the marriage, printing: *'Godmanchester, Sept. 21. Particular Baptist Chapel. George Ambrose to Mary Ann Simpson* [sic] *Harcock* [sic]*'* [**The Huntingdonshire Post**, Saturday, 3rd October 1908: page 8, column 8], Polly's husband was not a well man then and, indeed, it may already have been known that his remaining time of life was to be limited. At any event, he died (just two days before Christmas), from a heart condition which had been diagnosed three months earlier. What a sad and tragic happening, especially for Polly whose life seemed to be dogged by the deaths of those most close. Bravely, Polly stayed with her husband to the end; then, she must have fought her way through the Christmas period, including presenting herself before Mr. Scotney, the Registrar, at Huntingdon on Boxing Day.

Whenever it was that a grave plot was purchased for her dying or just–deceased husband, the opportunity was taken simultaneously of reserving space for Polly herself next to his, for the records of the Nonconformist Burial Ground in the Parish Churchyard of St. Mary the Virgin show this (and also show that at that time Eliza Jane Hercock reserved a space for herself next to Polly's – strongly presenting yet more evidence that Polly was her favourite niece). At that time, then, Polly must have had an expectation that she would come to lie near George ... eventually.

> The numbering scheme and chronology in the written burial records of the Nonconformist Burial Ground at Godmanchester suggest that Eliza Jane and Polly decided on making these grave plot reservations quite soon after the death of Susannah Hercock – which might suggest that it was the old lady's passing that concentrated minds on their owners' mortality and the fragility of human life.

Though Polly was to die many years after the chronological ending of this chapter in the overall story of the lives of the Hercocks, her expectation of burial at Godmanchester was never realised, for in later life she was to live contentedly in Needingworth, finally being buried there.

George Ambrose's burial (on 28th December [From the records of burials in the Nonconformist Burial Ground in the Parish Churchyard of St. Mary the Virgin, Godmanchester]) was eventually followed the erection of a headstone on which was inscribed:–

In loving memory of George Ambrose who died in the Lord Dec[r] 23rd 1908 aged 68 [sic] *years 'My times are in thy hand' Psalm 31.15.*

Information from a transcription of Godmanchester Monumental Inscriptions from the Nonconformist Burial Ground, is per the County Record Office, Huntingdon (now the Huntingdonshire Archives), and from the headstone itself. The age given is correct as taken from the headstone, but the latter appears erroneous as the death certificate (which agrees with George Ambrose's age given at the marriage only three months earlier) gives 60 years. It was on 18th August 2009 that I first found the headstone in person; it is still in very good condition (2011).

Grave memorial of Polly's husband, George Ambrose

Much of the emotional burden of supporting Polly must have fallen on her Aunt Eliza who had now seen the deaths of four relations in as many years. Her own strength of character and her unshakeable faith would have been the cornerstones of her capable person, enabling her to weather these losses and, simultaneously, give succour to others around her: she shared their pain as she bore her own.

◉ ◉ ◉ ◉ ◉ ◉ ◉ ◉ ◉ ◉ ◉ ◉ ◉ ◉ ◉ ◉ ◉ ◉ ◉ ◉

Some may come, some may go ...

In Dunstable, Charles James Hercock and his wife were, naturally, now some distance removed from their remaining 'HERCOCK' relations in Godmanchester, so visits between them had probably become less frequent. Their years in Potton had not been forgotten, though, and they kept up with friends there as best they could – but, again, distance may have proved something of an impediment to regular physical contact. Even more far removed, of course, were 'CJ's nephews in Essex, but even they kept contact through correspondence (as a surviving letter from much later proves).

Although 'CJ' had, clearly, generally enjoyed life in Potton, there must have been something more about Dunstable, and the Strict Baptist Chapel to which he and Annie gave their allegiance, that called him out, spiritually, in a way that had not previously been so. For, on Sunday, 27th September 1908 – just a few months after the couple had moved to the town where they lived above their Tea-Room and Bakery at 1 Church Street – 'CJ' underwent Believer's Baptism at the Chapel in St. Mary's Street, just behind the Market Square, and went on to be accepted as a Member there during the evening service on the following Sunday (Annie, too, became a Member at that time, her Membership being transferred from Potton). 'CJ's father and mother would have been immensely moved by this event.

A quarterly pew–rent at the Dunstable Strict Baptist Chapel was paid in 'CJ's name from July 1908. To begin with he had paid for three seats (for himself, his wife and their youngest son, Wilfred), but in 1914 he began paying for an entire pew, reverting to paying for three seats from 1918.

That Annie's Membership was transferred from Potton is the clinching piece of evidence that it was Mary Anne Hercock who joined the Potton Baptist Chapel in December 1894 (See the text on page 38).

Laurie and Rene Flowerday

Was 'CJ', perhaps, influenced in some way by his daughter Ruth's having taken this same step just the month before? Her Baptism had taken place in the Chapel at Maldon [From the **Membership Book of Maldon Baptist Church**], where she and Will had set up their first home. Ruth – having fallen pregnant in the autumn, not long after her Baptism – began to prepare herself and their home for their first–born, whilst Will became quite active in Chapel affairs (for instance, he was elected Auditor for the Baptist Chapel at Maldon, in February 1909). Irene Ruth Flowerday was born to the couple at 20 Fambridge Road, Maldon, on 7th June 1909; their second child, Laurence William, was born there on 5th August the following year.

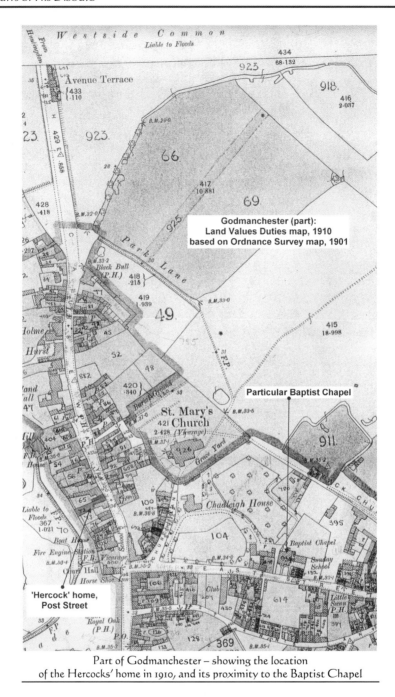

Part of Godmanchester – showing the location
of the Hercocks' home in 1910, and its proximity to the Baptist Chapel

It was in this year (1910) that Eliza Jane Hercock is known to have been the
tenant of one William Gadsby of Godmanchester, and lived in a house he owned
on the west side of Post Street, not far from its junction with East Street; her
tenancy entitled her, too, to one Common Right of grazing for animals on the
West Common!

Information here was extracted from the 1910 Land Values Duty Register for Godmanchester, held by the Huntingdonshire Archives (formerly Huntingdonshire Record Office). The Map (based on the latest (1901) Ordnance Survey), which accompanies the Register shows the precise position of the property in its surrounding area, the property being identified as Number 72 to accord with that Assessment Number in the Register. The Register and Map show that the adjoining property, Assessment Number 65, was in the occupancy of Mr. John Topham Gadsby and was also owned by William Gadsby.

This gives us an insight into where Eliza's mother and sister, Anna, (who, as we've seen, had been living with her in Post Street for some time hitherto) had been located (later evidence will confirm that eventually four 'HERCOCK' females had lived in this same house), as it appears the tenancy was of several years' standing. William Gadsby, Eliza's landlord, also lived in the town and was something of a local dignitary, being a Justice of the Peace, town Councillor and currently Deputy–Mayor (he'd been Mayor previously [From a plaque on the Town Hall at Godmanchester]); he was a Farmer, having been born in the parish circa 1848, son of John Topham Gadsby.

Kelly's Directory of Huntingdonshire, 1910, records William Gadsby J.P. living in Godmanchester, where he was Deputy–Mayor and Councillor (due to retire in 1912); and also records one John Topham Gadsby there. Earlier information about this family is from the 1881 Census of Godmanchester which shows William Gadsby, aged 33 years, a Farmer of 800 acres, living with his wife and children in West Street Farm House; and his father, John Topham Gadsby, aged 59 years, an Alderman, Merchant, Cattle Dealer and Farmer of 320 acres, widowed and living in Post Street. John Topham Gadsby appears to have been a son of an elder William Gadsby who'd been born in Godmanchester circa 1804, and at the 1881 Census was a widower living in Hemingford Grey, Huntingdonshire, where he was a Farmer. This elder William Gadsby clearly returned to Godmanchester ... where he died on 5th February 1885, aged 81 years – he'd attended the Godmanchester Particular Baptist Chapel for over 70 years, though never a member there [Information extracted from the **wrapper** of **The Gospel Standard**, March 1885]. Thus, it appears this 'GADSBY' family was of long standing locally and had a history of association with the Particular Baptist Chapel – from which we may infer the origin of Eliza Jane Hercock's connection with her landlord. There is no evident connection of this Godmanchester 'GADSBY' family with the family of Mr. John Gadsby, the well–known Baptist Publisher of the 19th Century, who'd been born in Manchester, Lancashire, circa 1809 (youngest son of a William Gadsby, preacher and hymn–writer) and who, after many years living in the London area, had moved to Hove, Sussex, by the time of the 1881 Census.

Another development in the family during 1910 saw the Baxters once more on the move, having been in Godmanchester some fourteen years – the longest period of settlement in any of the places they had ever lived, which must say a great deal for their overall contentment with the town. But the times were now changing in directions, and with a rapidity, they could neither bring themselves to favour or to comprehend, with Mary's mother and sister, Anna, having died and her younger sister, Susanna, having remarried and moved away. Furthermore, it was now time for William to retire from active business. William and Mary Baxter were only ever going to put themselves where they looked with approbation upon a Baptist Chapel of their Cause; this time they chose Yaxley, in Huntingdonshire, lying some 15½ miles north–east from Huntingdon and a few miles south of Peterborough, very near Norman Cross. The Friends at Godmanchester Chapel recorded in their

Sisters Susanna Markwell and Mary Hayes Baxter, circa 1909

Membership List that both William and Mary Baxter were *'Dismissed to Yaxley 1910'* – which means the couple had their Memberships formally transferred. [**Godmanchester Strict Baptist Church Book, 1882–1947**: Membership List, page 15]

The Strict Baptist Chapel in Yaxley, known as the 'Jireh Chapel', traced its origins to about the time that Mary's father had first moved his family to Peterborough on assuming the Pastorate at North Street. Indeed, the building of the Yaxley Chapel derived from the efforts of one George Speechley who had come out of Peterborough and opened his private house in the village for Prayer Meetings. Interest grew by degrees, giving Speechley encouragement and motivation to secure, enlarge and convert a local cottage into a Meeting House which eventually led to the erection of the Chapel, a purpose–built building, in 1860. Lacking all external adornment, this building was plain *in extremis*. However, it was to prove a worrying encumbrance to the small Cause in Yaxley, for a mortgage taken out to enable its construction proved to be a serious burden under the weight of which the Friends were still labouring when the Baxters joined them. At the 1911 Census William and Mary were recorded in Yaxley, both now retired; they were living in the Chapel House, Chapel Lane – which may suggest they were occupying (possibly as 'Housekeepers') the residence for a Minister associated with the village's Strict Baptist Chapel. As this couple would have been generous in their financial support of their new Friends, it's likely their arrival on the scene helped the Yaxley Chapel's cash flow sufficiently to allow the debt to be cleared – which finally was achieved in 1913. [**Ralph F. Chambers, 1963**: pages 121 & 122] As the Chapel then closed, presumably through lack of adequate support, especially with its history of financial worries, it was at that point that William and Mary returned to Godmanchester ... in June.

> Published for The Strict Baptist Historical Society, 1963, Volume Four of the series **The Strict Baptist Chapels of England: The Industrial Midlands** by Ralph F. Chambers is herein cited as '**Ralph F. Chambers, 1963**'.

Mary Hayes Baxter's health had been in decline for a while, to such a degree – as she was approaching her seventy–fifth year – as to lead her to feel the end of her life might be drawing near. So, it was time to return to more familiar territory and prepare herself for what was to come. Friends at Godmanchester Chapel received news of the couple's return with gladness, and unreservedly welcomed them back to the fold. Part of the business of a Church Meeting held on 12th December 1913 was to consider the Baxters' request to have their Memberships reinstated here, which was duly done. The written record reads as follows: '*The Pastor said that as Mr & Mrs Baxter had returned to reside in Godmanchester he thought they might be reinstated as members with us without the usual formalities. It was unanimously agreed to.*' [**Godmanchester Strict Baptist Church Book, 1882–1947**: page 116] The Pastor was still, of course, Mr. Joseph Oldfield, the Baxters' old friend and mentor whose ministry Mary particularly favoured and enjoyed.

Mary may have had ample cause to consider her future, for only the preceding year she had received news that her next younger sister, Lucy Ann Underwood, had died at Sheffield. The death had occurred on 29th February – the year was a leap year – at 14 Brighton Terrace Road (in the Ecclesall district); here her daughter, Helen, comforted her mother at the end, attending the Register Office the following day to register the death. Lucy, who appeared to have been lodging at this address to be near her daughter, had been suffering from 'degenerative disease of the circulatory system'. She was buried in Sheffield's Crookes Cemetery on the afternoon of Monday, 4th March 1912, following a funeral service (which, it appears, was held in the Cemetery Chapel).

> A death and funeral announcement appeared in the **Sheffield Daily Telegraph** of 2nd March.

> Lucy Ann Underwood lies in Grave Number 2491 (in Section D, General, of the Cemetery). Section D is in the unconsecrated part of the Cemetery; the Grave Plot Register shows that the grave was not purchased by anyone, meaning it could have been used as a communal grave for burials of unrelated people; there is, consequently, unlikely ever to have been a memorial erected at the grave. Information from Sheffield City Council Bereavement Services and Sheffield Archives.

Reading between the lines of the Obituary that Lucy's son, William Henry, penned, one can comprehend the nature of some of the difficulties that this daughter had caused her parents and some of her siblings (not to mention her offspring), and that she had been something of a loner. This Obituary appeared in **The Gospel Standard**:–

> On Feb. 29th, 1912, Lucy Ann Underwood, widow, aged 72 years. My mother was a daughter of the late Mr. H. Hercock, Particular Baptist minister. She had many troubles. She was for the last few years a valuable member of the Strict Baptist church at Sheffield. Her faith in Christ, both in temporal and spiritual matters, was very strong ; and she died having no confidence in the flesh, but trusting in that God who had led her through so many difficulties and trials in safety. W. H. Underwood.
>
> [**The Gospel Standard**, 1912: page 282]

Just what had brought Lucy Ann to Sheffield is not known – she was no longer working, so it may have been to accompany her daughter, Helen Susannah, who, presumably, was now supporting her seventy–plus mother in her time of failing health.

> Until late October 2008, I knew only that Helen Underwood's second forename initial was 'S'. During detailed studies being carried out in the writing of this account, I was suddenly to educe that the most probable name based on this would have been 'Susannah' – after her 'HERCOCK' grandmother. Within less than a week from then I discovered the following entry in White's Directory of Sheffield, 1911: '*Underwood Miss Helen Susannah, 139 Hadfield street'*. Corroboration that this was the daughter of Lucy Ann Underwood came from both the 1911 Census and the presence in Sheffield of her future husband, Edwin Toogood, as well as her mother's death there the following year.

There does not seem to have been a particularly robust reason for Lucy to have come to Sheffield on grounds of the lure of a Baptist Chapel or minister, for the city does not appear to have offered Strict Baptists a strong base. The earliest evidence of a Strict Baptist Cause in the city indicates first foundation as late as 1893, which arose from preliminary, seeding meetings of a small number of like–minded folk in a Mission Room. They did not last long here, however, for in 1894 they moved to Zion Chapel in Barrack Lane for worship, and were still there in 1897. What happened to this group is not known – whether it formed the backbone of the next assemblage to appear, in 1908, or whether the latter was from different roots, is unknown. This later collection of Friends, meeting in a room at Brookhill (or Brook Hill), launched an appeal for funds that year, with the result that by 1909 a Chapel, known as 'Mount Olivet', in a building which had belonged to another religious movement, had been secured; this was in Heavygate Road, Walkley. Though the building needed much work, it was gradually rendered suitable for the worship of God. [**Ralph F. Chambers (unpublished manuscript), 1950s**] As there was no settled minister, it was solely by Supply preaching that this Chapel was serviced. Given the similar chronology of this latter Chapel to the time of arrival of Lucy Ann and Helen in Sheffield, it would appear likely that it was to this group of Friends that they attached themselves ... in which case this Cause would have qualified as *'the Strict Baptist Church at Sheffield'* – to which William Underwood refers in his brief Obituary to his mother. It is entirely probable that Lucy Ann and Helen had come to Sheffield as early as circa 1904, as White's Directory of Sheffield for 1905 lists a *'Miss Ellen Underwood'* at 16 Reliance Place – this entry could relate to Helen, in fact; and, certainly, Trade Directories of Derby (their former place of residence) covering the period 1903 to 1908 show no presence there of either Lucy Ann, her daughter, or her son William Henry.

> Information on the history of Strict Baptist Chapels in Sheffield is from **Ralph F. Chambers (unpublished manuscript), 1950s**. Mr. David J. Woodruff, Librarian of The Strict Baptist Historical Society, tells me he has found no reference to a group meeting in Zion Chapel after 1897, but that in both **The Gospel Standard** and **The Christian's Pathway** references to Sheffield mention 'Mount Olivet' or its predecessor, 'Ebenezer', at Brook Hill (such references continue up to the 1980s, when the Chapel appears to have closed). On the strength of this additional information, it would seem that this is the Chapel to which Lucy Ann Underwood was attached.
>
> My reason for postulating the reference to 'Miss Ellen Underwood' actually means Helen Susannah Underwood is based on evidence from the 1911 Census and Sheffield Trade Directory cited earlier; the Directory establishes that it was the unmarried Helen (often interchangeably used with, or even mistaken as, 'Ellen') under whose name the Directory entry was placed; but the 1911 Census is the clinching piece of evidence, showing Helen Susannah Underwood (a Shop Assistant) as the Head of the household at 139 Hadfield Street which she shared with her mother Lucy Ann and brother William Henry (whose occupation is recorded as a 'Sales Man Collector').

With her mother's death still so vivid in her memory, Helen Underwood's marriage to Edwin Toogood the following year must have been another of those family occasions carrying hugely mixed emotions. Her husband (whom the 1901 Census revealed as a Civil Servant employed by the Post Office as a 'Town Postman' – at the 1881 Census he'd been designated a 'Letter Carrier'), was a native of Sheffield who had had a previous marriage; but he'd been widowed upon the death of his first wife, Louisa, in 1907. Before that, Edwin and Louisa had lived at 12 Brighton Terrace Road, where (after Louisa's death) Edwin had continued to reside until, in all likelihood, Helen moved in there with him shortly before their marriage – so that she could be right next–door to the property in which her mother was housed during the approach to death. After Lucy Ann had died, and despite the physical distance which separated Helen Toogood from her Aunt Eliza Jane Hercock, they evidently managed to maintain some contact.

> The Post Office remained part of the British Civil Service until the 1980s, and was the largest single employer in the country at that time.
>
> White's Directory of Sheffield, 1905, at 12 Brighton Terrace Road (off Spring Vale Road): *'Toogood Edwin, postman'*. White's Directory of Sheffield, 1911: *'Toogood Edwin, 12 Brighton Terrace Road (off Spring Vale Road)'*.

There'd been another marriage, too: this one a couple of years earlier and nearer home for the spinster Eliza. Her other niece, Polly Ambrose, having recovered from the distress of the loss of her first husband, George, had latterly been courted by an old friend of the family in the person of Robert Thompson Senescall. Mr. Senescall, who was an affluent businessman (at that time principally a Miller and Baker) and proprietor of a family firm in Needingworth – a small hamlet within the parish of Holywell–cum–Needingworth – had himself been widowed, having lived through the horror of his first wife's suicide. Ida Mary, having borne her husband three sons and a daughter between 1893 and 1902, took her own life whilst mentally disturbed, at the young age of 39 years; the couple had been married some sixteen years. It was on Saturday, 30th April 1910 that she jumped into the 'Hundred Feet River about one mile from Sutton Chain Public House', drowning herself in so doing. An Inquest into the incident was held at Ely on the Monday, presided over by the Coroner for the Southern District of the Isle of Ely, Mr. G. M. Hall, who issued the certificate enabling her death to be registered the following day. The **Ely Weekly Guardian & Cambs. Weekly News** of 6th May published an account of the incident and Inquest, revealing that the deceased had left a sad suicide note, exonerating her husband fully from all culpability – on the contrary, the note praised him as '... *a dear, true, good husband'*. Ida had a history of low self–esteem and depression, having previously been treated by the family doctor who gave evidence at the Inquest. A headstone, rare for this family – who did not generally subscribe to such memorials at their graves – was eventually erected at Ida Mary's last resting place in the burial ground of Needingworth Strict Baptist Chapel.

With several young children and a thriving business to oversee, it was understandable that the grieving widower, then in his early forties, should put his sorrows – however deeply felt – to one side in the interests of his children, and make room in his life for a new wife at the earliest opportunity. So it was that, after what they must have judged an acceptable interval, despite its overt brevity, Robert Thompson Senescall and Mary Ann Sawyer Ambrose were married at the Huntingdon Register Office just a few days after Christmas 1911. The day being a Saturday, they could attend Chapel together in Needingworth the following day as man and wife. The Strict Baptist Chapel at Needingworth thus became Polly's regular place of worship, the building here having been erected in 1861 to replace the old one after it had begun to crumble – literally – about the heads of its Friends! [**Ralph F. Chambers, 1963**: page 123] Polly took on the difficult rôle of stepmother to her new husband's young children, but soon

Polly Senescall in later life, with two of her step–grandchildren

won them over with her gentle charms and kindly manner; whilst giving the children the nearest to their own mother's love, in turn Polly was to reap the great affection of not just her husband, but also his children and, so, finally found peace, contentment and a settled home within this special marriage upon which she had entered rather late in life and, perhaps, beyond the age at which she'd thought it likely.

Retired from retail trade, her Aunt Eliza Jane who, up to this time, had had Polly living with her at Post Street (the 1911 Census shows the two of them sharing the same residence, where both are said to be of 'Private Means') suddenly must have felt the cold stab of loneliness deep inside as her home, 'til then shared with one or other of her close relations, became her own alone. Though her aloneness may have been masked to some extent by seasonal festive celebrations and visits to and from other family and friends, it would have been after nightfall, when the house finally fell silent as the last visitor left, that Eliza would have been most acutely aware of her new, and – perhaps – not so welcome, situation. The bitter emptiness of the winter darkness would have closed in around her. Providentially, Eliza's sole occupancy of her home was relatively short–lived because, when the Baxters returned to the town in 1913, they came to share her abode in Post Street.

Their shared home, adjoined by and squeezed between a traditional two–storey, double–fronted house and a three–storey Georgian town–house, was of modest proportions with a front door which opened directly on to the street ... this would have been, in the days when she ran her Toy–Shop from these premises, the door leading into the shop, for upon entering and to the right of this door was a large shop–window fronting on to the public footpath. So it was here that her wares would have been displayed to passers–by. The rear garden extended down to the River Ouse, an idyllic setting sporting ducks and other water fowl, on the opposite bank of which were graceful weeping willows and open water–meadows. A stone's throw farther along Post Street (in the direction away from Huntingdon and towards Cambridge) lay the Town Hall; there, at a junction of several thoroughfares, East Street branched off and, within a matter of just two–hundred yards or so, passed by the Particular Baptist Chapel. So, the location of the Hercocks' home couldn't have been more central or convenient for both Chapel, shopping and business.

The house in Post Street formerly occupied by the Hercocks

It was about this time (1913) that 'CJ' and Mary Annie in Dunstable moved their home and business into new, larger premises (very probably purpose–built for them) in the town's Great Northern Road. With ample domestic and working accommodation, this was to provide both a comfortable family home and efficient base for the running of their family Bakery which was already forging quite a name in the town and surrounding villages. In fact, before this move the Bakery had attracted such a volume of trade that 'CJ' had had to find help – with great good fortune that had been forthcoming in the person of his son, Bertram, who had not taken to the trade of Hatter and Hosier. Bertram, then about 24 years old, had come to live once more with his parents some time around 1910, specifically to help them out, and had committed himself to the St. Mary's Street Strict Baptist Chapel by being Baptised there that December, following this up by becoming a Member on New Year's Day 1911. Little could have gladdened the spirits of his parents more than having their gentle, good–humoured son with them both at home, at work and at Chapel. Riding around town and nearby villages on bread delivery rounds in their horse–drawn cart – on whose side was the proud sign 'HERCOCK'S HYGIENIC BAKERY' – 'CJ' and Bertram cut a dashing sight smartly turned out in suits and bowler hats! Bertram, the second oldest of 'CJ' and Annie's boys, had supplanted his older brother, Charles Ernest, as natural heir and successor to their father because Ernie had gone on from times at Potton to make quite a nuisance of himself, causing much anguish to his parents and simultaneously distancing himself from most of his siblings. Annie's favourite – 'CJ' and Annie's youngest son, Wilfred Henry – also lived with them while he was completing his schooling locally.

A couple of years earlier, the 1911 Census recorded that the household of Charles James Hercock (then still at 1 Church Street, Dunstable) included not only 'CJ' and his wife Mary Annie, but also their two sons Bertram (an Assistant Baker) and Wilfred Henry (a Scholar).

As it happens, the rebellious Ernie had married in the mid–summer of 1910, but his wife, a Londoner, was a woman not much liked by the 'HERCOCK' family who found her rather vulgar. Having wed in the Congregational Church in Camberwell, the couple lived for a few years thereafter in Lewisham, where

Brothers Bertram, Albert and Wilfred Henry Hercock as young men

they had two boys. By this time Ernie had jettisoned all contact with the printing trade to which his father had originally introduced him whilst living in Potton, and had become an employed Baker.

At the 1911 Census, meanwhile, Josiah's legitimate first wife, Lucretia, was still living with her younger, unmarried son, Sydney, at the same address in Upper Tooting where they'd been some five years earlier, so Lucretia's possible premonition of an early death had not turned out in reality; she now kept home for her son who worked as a Municipal Engineer's Clerk. And Lucretia's elder son, Clerk and Collector for the Dispensary, John Henry Hurlock, and his wife, Ada, were living where John worked at Hull & Sculcoates Dispensary, North Boulevard, Hull, with their three children (Raymond, Nellie Lucretia and Clifford) whose ages ranged from 5 to 2 years.

~ ~

A terrible blight was about to strike the world in August 1914 when the First World War began. The Hercocks were not to be immune from war scarring, though – miraculously, perhaps – their ranks were to be thinned far less than those of many other families up and down Britain. However, on the scale of personal family tragedies the Hercocks were to experience devastation and great pain just a few months before the commencement of wider hostilities ... when Mary Hayes Baxter died. The stark terseness of the Godmanchester Baptist Chapel's Membership List, simply recording against her name '*died Jun* [sic] *24 1914 at G*[odmanchester]' [**Godmanchester Strict Baptist Church Book, 1882-1947**: Membership List, page 15], concealed the reality of streams of bitter tears expressed by those who had known and loved her as one of the most gentle and genteel of family womenfolk, clean and pure in spirit, to have crossed their paths. The hurt felt at her passing would have been widely shared as if by angels mourning her demise as one of their own.

That many had witnessed Mary's decline, from the time when she and William still lived at Yaxley, will have diminished not at all the shock of her sudden death at home on 24th January. She was in her seventy–sixth year. William, her ever–devoted husband, was with his wife to the last, comforting and praying with her. It is hard to imagine the depths of his grief as he was suddenly bereft of the partner with whom he had shared so much since their marriage in Peterborough over fifty years earlier. Of all the pairings of the progeny of Henry and Susannah Hercock, it was this union of Mary with William Baxter which was the most long–lived. Childless though it was, there was much fruit and sweetness which came from this tight–knit matrimonial bond in so many other ways. But now it was over. For Mary, death came as a release from the most dreadful bronchitis imaginable, the strain of which had brought about heart failure. There'd been little anyone, even the doctor, could do except watch and wait, flinching with each bout of the rasping cough, with increasing awareness that the end would not be long in coming.

The public announcement of Mary's death glossed over the agonising symptoms of her final few days, framing the context somewhat differently for the benefit of the newspaper's readers and others not so well–known to the 'HERCOCK' family:–

> GODMANCHESTER   Death of Mrs. Baxter – We regret to record the death of Mrs. Mary H. Baxter, wife of Mr. William Baxter, daughter of the late Mr. Hurcock *[sic]*, of Potton, Beds., sister of Miss Hurcock *[sic]*, Godmanchester, Mrs. Markwell, Sutton, late *[sic]* of Ely, and Mrs. George *[sic]* Duddington, of Peterborough, which took place unexpectedly at Post–street Godmanchester, one hour after midnight on Saturday last. Although deceased saw her 75th year, she had not a robust constitution, and used to remark that she wondered she lived so long. She attended the Particular Baptist Chapel, of which denomination she was a member, on Sunday morning, January 11th, in company with her husband, but on her return she complained very much of the cold, which appeared to have had an effect on her, and she regretted she went out that morning. She retired to bed as usual, but was unable to rise the following morning, and subsequently medical aid was called in. Nothing serious was apprehended, and at intervals she seemed to rally, but on Friday afternoon symptoms were apparent, and it was feared the end was approaching, and death took place as stated. Mr. Baxter was in business at George–street, Huntingdon, at a fancy repository, from which he retired some time ago and went to reside at Yaxley. He, however, came to Godmanchester during the course of last year and he and Mrs. Baxter resided with her sister, Miss Hurcock *[sic]*, in Post–street. The funeral took place at Godmanchester on Thursday.
>
> [**The Huntingdonshire Post**, 30th January 1914: page 4, column 7]

This newspaper report carries several errors, which are: (1) the phrase '*late of Ely*' should read '*Isle of Ely*'; (2) the reference to '*Mrs. George Duddington*' should read '*Mrs. Joseph Duddington*'; and (3) both Mr. & Mrs. Baxter had come to Godmanchester together during the course of the last year to reside with Mary's sister in Post Street.

There would have been a large turnout for the funeral in Godmanchester Particular Baptist Chapel that 29th January [From the records of burials in the

Nonconformist Burial Ground in the Parish Churchyard of St. Mary the Virgin, Godmanchester], and afterwards to witness the lowering of Mary's coffin into the grave which had been prepared in the Nonconformist Burial Ground in the Parish Churchyard of St. Mary the Virgin. The grave was not far from those of Mary's mother and sister, Anna.

A memorial headstone, later erected at the grave, bore the inscription:–

In Loving Memory of Mary H Baxter, died Jany 24th 1914 Aged 75 years. '
Adoring saints around Him stand, And thrones and powers before Him fall.
The God shines gracious through the man, And sheds sweet glories on them
all.'

> I discovered Mary Hayes Baxter's grave during my first visit to the Parish Churchyard of St. Mary the Virgin, Godmanchester, on 13th June 2002. It is now (2011) in poor condition, its surface spalling badly.

The Gospel Standard carried the following Obituary:–

MARY HAYES BAXTER, of Godmanchester, entered her eternal rest on Jan. 24th, 1914, aged 75 years. She was the eldest daughter of the late Henry Hercock, Baptist minister.* He often said she was sanctified before her birth. The Lord began a work of grace in her heart early in life, and so kept her from much outward evil. At that time she lived at Hambleton, a village near Oakham, and sat under Mr. Philpot, whose ministry was used in cutting her up inwardly, and showing her her need of a Saviour. Afterwards Mr. Godwin came there to preach, and so entered into her case and the place she was then in, that she felt much encouraged to hope it was the Lord's work in her soul. After that, in hearing various ministers and feeling much liberty in prayer, she became more settled in her mind, and confirmed that it was the work of the Holy Spirit in her heart ; and afterwards was so blessed that in 1860 she expressed to one of her sisters that she had received the Spirit of adoption. In 1862 she married, and spiritually travailed in birth for the deliverance of her husband. One evening the Lord gave her the words, " He is able, He is willing ; " and so graciously fulfilled them that they were both baptised by her father at Peterborough, in Feb., 1863. Before her last illness, while residing at Yaxley, she was much impressed that she should not live long, and wished to return to Godmanchester to sit under Mr. Oldfield's ministry again, having from time to time before felt it to be life and power to her soul. She was especially blessed on one occasion, when he preached from, " Thine eyes shall see the King in His beauty " (Isa. xxxiii. 17). The way being opened, she came to Godmanchester in June, 1913 ; and many times she spoke of hearing with profit and pleasure, so that it became evident to others that the Lord was ripening her for the end ; and it was so. She took to her bed ten days before she departed. One day she said to a friend, " I just want the Lord to give me one more manifestation, and then take me home ; " and the next day the Lord gave her the answer from hymn 481, verse 4:
" Adoring saints before Him stand,
/ And thrones and powers before

Him fall ; / The God shines gracious through the Man, / And sheds sweet glories on them all. " Shortly after this foretaste and glimpse of heaven, the Lord came and took her to Himself most peacefully. She had an attack of the heart, breathed two or three short breaths, and was gone.

Mr. Oldfield being laid up at the time, Mr. Short, an old friend of hers, came and committed her remains to the grave, in sure and certain hope of the resurrection unto eternal life, through our Lord Jesus Christ. W. BAXTER. (*Footnote:* * See a letter by Mr. Hercock, in Dec. No., p. 550.)

[**The Gospel Standard**, 1915: pages 42 & 43]

> It is from the foregoing reference to Mary's having '*sat under Mr. Philpot*' whilst living at Hambleton, Rutland, when still young that we know the 'HERCOCK' family gave their allegiance, in those far–off days of the late 1830s and early 1840s, to The Factory Chapel at Oakham (as the original Providence Chapel had colloquially been known due to its origins in a disused former factory building). The Obituary also makes apparent that Mr. Thomas Godwin was an old friend from those far–off days in Rutland.

† †

So it came to pass that the 'HERCOCK' family lost one of its most beloved and constant members. As the first–born of all the progeny of Henry and Susannah, Mary held a special place within the group and enjoyed a particular respect among her siblings – after the passing of their parents, it was the loss of Mary that most deeply affected those remaining, casting long shadows over the residual times of their own lives.

There are several points to note particularly. The reference (in the newspaper report) to death having occurred '*... one hour after midnight on Saturday,*' taken with the later reference '*... on Friday afternoon symptoms were apparent, and ... death took place as stated,*' would seem to indicate that death occurred at about 1 a.m. (01:00 hours) on Saturday, 24th January (which is the date given on the death certificate). The death certificate gives 76 years as her age, but she would not have reached that age until 21st June 1914. William, Mary's husband, described himself as '*formerly a Stationer and Fancy Shopkeeper*' when he went to register her death at Huntingdon on Monday, 26th January. Most curious and puzzling of all is the fact that Mary's brother, Charles James Hercock, is not mentioned in the newspaper report even though Mary was still in contact with him; this omission, taken with the repeated misspelling, '*Hurcock*', would appear to indicate that the subject–matter for the report was not given by any family member, but, rather, a close friend at Chapel who knew the family and certain recent events in their ranks reasonably well, yet not that well as to be aware that Mary had a brother living in Dunstable. Since Mary's husband, William, was the elder brother of 'CJ's wife, Mary Annie (née Baxter), the omission is peculiarly disconcerting. Finally, no public Will has ever been discovered in Mary Baxter's name; it must be presumed, then, that she had insufficient assets to her name to have warranted such a document and, moreover, those of any significance which she had possessed had been passed before her death to her husband and a few close relations, as gifts.

⊚ ⊚ ⊚ ⊚ ⊚ ⊚ ⊚ ⊚ ⊚ ⊚ ⊚ ⊚ ⊚ ⊚ ⊚ ⊚ ⊚ ⊚ ⊚

The Final Chapter

William Baxter and his sister–in–law, Eliza Jane Hercock, of course were the two to bear the brunt of Mary's death. Living in the same house at Godmanchester, and despite their advanced ages (William was about 74 years, Eliza just about a year younger), the fact that Eliza was a spinster may have been of some concern to William as the took account of how other folk might perceive their relationship. But, in any case, for him to continue in this same house, in this same town, worshipping in the same Baptist Chapel – as he had done for so many years gone – in which he had day–by–day, week–by–week, seen his dear wife and soulmate, quickly turned out to be something he couldn't bear. All the memories, his imaginings of hearing Mary's voice around the home, the visual images that entered his mind, her touch – all these sharpened his grief to the point where he had to leave.

It was to nearby Houghton he took himself, his departure thence once more leaving Eliza to contemplate life on her own, rattling round in the house which had seen so many of her dear family members come and go over the years since she had first set foot in Godmanchester to live. The weight of nostalgia must, at times, have been hard to bear, for not only had Eliza seen so many of her own flesh and blood pass on during the recent ten years or so, but she had begun to notice that around her Friends at Chapel were more aged than young, numbers declining, and The Word no longer sought so assiduously as in those far–off days when she and her father had been wont to discuss and debate together the paths of righteousness and their shared faith. Those were the days when her body and mind had possessed a vigour and verve she no longer knew, when she and her sisters could rejoice in each other's company and benefit from the knowledgeable, wise counsel of their parents. Now, as Eliza sat by the fireside, lost in silent reverie of the joys of days past, stung from time to time by the melancholy of painful happenings within the family – seeing the whole panoply of life swirling and sweeping past her again in replay – the realisation must gradually have come to her that the fragility of human life could mean only one thing: that she, too, was now in that realm of 'three score years and ten' when the Lord whom she still praised so faithfully might call her Home at any time. Sure in the knowledge that a happy and peaceful eternal life would be hers, she perhaps now wished for the day, and relished its advent.

Though that day was not to be long in the coming, Eliza had yet to witness a few more markers of time in the earthly annals of her family; but she prepared herself, nevertheless, in drawing up her own Will on 17th December 1915 (it was sometime later that an Affidavit of Due Execution was to be filed, to the effect that the Will had been signed on the specified date). As was so characteristic of the woman, it was her closest family members who were foremost in her mind that day and to whom she Willed her entire Estate; they were her only living brother Charles James Hercock of Dunstable; her sisters Susanna Markwell of Sutton, Ely, and Helen Letitia Duddington of Peterborough; and two of her nieces, Mary Ann Senescall of Needingworth and Helen Toogood of Sheffield. The same five were appointed her joint Executors and Executrices; and the Will – a plain and simple document of few lines – was witnessed by Robert Thompson Senescall and his son Stanley Charles Robert Senescall.

It is sadly ironic that on this day for preparing her Will, her sister Susanna's husband, William Markwell, died at his home at Sutton.

From the pages of **The Gospel Standard** we read that:–

William Markwell, of Sutton, Ely, died Dec. 17th, 1915, aged 79 years. He was called by grace when a young man, and was deeply tried and exercised both in spiritual and providential things. The Bible, "Gospel Standard," and Gadsby's hymn book, were the books he most prized. He and his wife joined the church at Sutton in the year 1887 ; she died in 1895. Before he died he asked the Lord to give him something to meditate and to rest on, and was answered with, "I am thy God, and will still give thee aid." These words were very sweet and precious to him until, soon after, he passed peacefully away, we feel assured to be for ever with the Lord. He leaves a widow, who was a daughter of the late Mr. Henry Hercock, Baptist minister, and a family to mourn his loss. He was buried by Mr. Wills, of St. Ives, in the Baptist chapel burying–ground, at Sutton, Isle of Ely. J. A. Parish.

[**The Gospel Standard**, 1916: page 331]

What a bleak, down–in–the–dumps Christmas poor Susanna must have had. Though a death is never a joyful event, to have it happen at the dawn of the Christmas festive season forevermore tends to cast a shadow of gloom over that otherwise special, celebratory time of year. Consoling each other, the two sisters, Eliza Jane and Susanna, both now in their seventies, perhaps spent the time together at Godmanchester, ruminating over both temporal and spiritual matters of relevance to their lives – as well as decrying the horrors of warfare which were daily becoming apparent as thousands of young British and British Empire soldiers' lives were being squandered in France and Belgium. This was to be the sisters' last Christmas together, for Eliza's turn to be called by her Maker came in the spring following.

It was Wednesday, 28th March when her spirit departed the earthly body. Warning signs had been evident in the weeks and days leading up to her actual death, as there'd been time for her sister, Helen Letitia, to come from Peterborough to be with Eliza at her demise. It was a final, fatal stroke that took the last vestiges of life from her – the details are no better put than in the newspaper report which appeared on the Friday of that week:–

GODMANCHESTER Death of Miss Hercock.–We regret to record the death of Miss Eliza Jane Hercock, which took place suddenly on Tuesday at her residence, Post–street. Deceased had one or two serious seizures some months ago, but seemed to have overcome them in great measure. She attended the morning and evening services at the Particular Baptist Chapel on Sunday. Miss Hercock was a daughter of the late Pastor Hercock of Potton, Beds., who used occasionally to preach at Godmanchester. She spent her younger days for some years at Cirencester, where she took a deep interest in religious work as a Sunday School teacher and Bible Class leader, and received a presentation on leaving. She came to Godmanchester more than 20 years ago, and kept a fancy repository at the house where she died, but she retired from business some time since. Deceased was a member of the Particular Baptist Chapel here, and an occasional teacher in the Sunday School. Four members of the family have died in this house, viz.: Miss Hercock and Mrs. Baxter (sisters), Mrs. Hercock (mother), and the one who now has died. Deceased was 75 years old. Two sisters survive.

[**The Huntingdonshire Post**, 31st March 1916: page 2, column 6]

Once again it was Helen who had the unenviable task of registering the death of another of her sisters. This time, though, the job was probably the more difficult and emotionally demanding for there was another, even less pleasant, task to be undertaken and which now loomed over her. With the death of Eliza, the house in Post Street which had been the 'HERCOCK' women's shared home for over twenty years had to be cleared and handed back to the landlord. Attending to this matter, sorting clothing, personal possessions, furniture and the myriad other items which – even in those relatively more abstemious times – folk tended to acquire through their lifetimes, is likely to have been shared between Susanna and Helen; even Charles James could have come over to Godmanchester from Dunstable on at least one visit to give his opinions on certain items and to take for himself those few small, highly–prized mementoes which one sees as such personifications of the beloved deceased. This brother of Eliza not being mentioned in the newspaper report would appear to indicate that the subject–matter for the report was not given by any family member, but, rather, a close friend at Chapel who was unaware of, or had momentarily overlooked, 'CJ's existence in Dunstable; in all probability this was Pastor Joseph Oldfield who would have been one of only a very few to have known sufficient of Eliza's earlier life to include such detail as is given in the newspaper account.

Out of respect for the deceased, none of this sorting and sifting of the contents of the home would have been begun before they'd committed her remains to the soil. Mourning deeply the passing of the final 'HERCOCK' inhabitant of Godmanchester, the solemn funeral service in the Baptist Chapel on Monday, 3rd April must have been especially poignant. The family was bidding 'Farewell' to one of their foremost motivating and most loved representatives, the Baptist Friends were marking the departure of another of their long–serving Members who had shown a special commitment to the Cause here, while friends and acquaintances from the area were paying last respects to one who had been well–known around Godmanchester (and in nearby Huntingdon) through her business activities. The burial which followed saw Eliza's mortal remains interred near her mother and sisters (and immediately adjacent her late brother–in–law, George Ambrose), where all could continue in the afterlife to share the good company they'd enjoyed with each other in earth–bound life.

Finally, against the name of 'Eliza Jane Hercock' there was marked in the Membership List in the **Church Book** of the Godmanchester Strict Baptist Chapel: *'Died in the Lord March 28.1916'*. [**Godmanchester Strict Baptist**

Church Book, 1882–1947: Membership List, page 15] In actuality, and – even more – symbolically, this was the closure of the worldly story of the Hercocks at Godmanchester: that quintessentially Strict Baptist group of Victorian ladies, prim and proper in their attire and deportment, cautious and frugal in their habits, measured and particular in their speech, utterly devoted to their faith ... attributes all which had made them so immediately noticeable around the town, so obviously eccentric in the eyes of the many, such outstanding characters in truth. Of these folk the tangible relics given to the town and community they'd loved were to be their tombstones solemnly standing in the tranquility of the Burial Ground amongst those of countless others, most to us strangely anonymous, where the latest to join them, Eliza Jane, is immortalised in the words:–

> *In loving memory of Eliza Jane Hercock, beloved daughter of the late Henry Hercock, who fell asleep March 28, 1916 Aged 74 years. 'Precious in the sight of the Lord is the death of his saints.'*

> I discovered Eliza Jane Hercock's grave during my first visit to the Parish Churchyard of St. Mary the Virgin, Godmanchester, on 13th June 2002. The headstone is in moderately good condition now (2011). [Photograph: see page C6]

Indeed a saint. A good woman who devoted herself to her Baptist faith which filled her soul and which she put at the true heart of her life; and also to her family, some members of which she unstintingly supported and cared for through thick and thin, working to maintain those of her kinfolk who were less able than herself. She'd captured the heart of her father from an early age, won the respect and appreciation of her mother through the later years of their shared companionship, and won the admiration of her siblings for the manner in which she conducted herself: especially for her perceptive, intelligent approach to life and earning living through the way she ran her Toy–Shop. The family of the Hercocks would have whispered her parting from them with a prayer for her soul, just as the company of all saints would have greeted her arrival in their midst with reverent approbation.

Now, at her ending, all that she left on earth was again given to the most cherished of her surviving blood relations – shared between those five whom she had named in her Will. Given that Eliza Jane Hercock had been such a loyal stalwart of the Strict Baptist Cause and a devoted daughter and sibling to her familial kin, it is sadly remiss that no–one saw fit to pen an obituary of her for publication in some relevant quarter of the religious press.

Probate was shortly granted, on 18th April, the formal, legal and unpunctuated statement naming *'Charles James Hercock of Great Northern Road Dunstable in the County of Bedford Baker brother Susanna Markwell of Sutton in the Isle of Ely in the County of Cambridge widow and Helen Lettitia [sic] Duddington of Olive House Walpole Street in the City of Peterborough (wife of Joseph Duddington) sisters and Mary Ann Senescall of Rose Villa Needingworth near Saint Ives in the County of Huntingdon (wife of Robert Thompson Senescall)* and Helen Toogood of 12 Brighton Terrace Villa Spring Vale Sheffield in the County of York (wife of Edwin Toogood) nieces of deceased the executors ...' The Estate was valued at £779 7s. 3d. (Gross), £10 17s. 3d. (Net). The large difference between the two valuations is indicative of the necessary settlement of outstanding debts, possibly including taxes, so the beneficiaries of her Will received very little – in terms of purely monetary worth – each.

> The Estate valuations are broadly equivalent, by today's values, to £30,000 (Gross), £400 (Net).

As Eliza's brother and two sisters took their leave of each other to return to their respective homes, they must have been acutely aware of their frail mortality and mutual separation. Though of the same blood, fate had ensured that these three remaining siblings were the least close as a group, having little in common nowadays apart from their mutual origins and genetic inheritance. Of spiritual matters, it was their Baptist faith which they still shared, yet in their advancing years it could not unite them in the flesh over the geographical divide that put them at the apices of the slim triangle: Dunstable (in the south) some fifty miles – as the crow flies – from Peterborough (in the north) and some forty miles from Sutton (in the east), and the latter some twenty miles from Peterborough (to the north–west). They were now to go their separate ways, no longer amalgamated by the binding forces which had been exercised from Godmanchester during the lives of those who had lately passed on.

Susanna Markwell, at Sutton, was the most isolated for she had no offspring of her own and no longer a husband either. Whether she'd retained the vivacity and drive of her earlier days, and now relied on them to buoy her spirits in these days of the flagging flesh, or whether she felt the loneliness of her alienation from her blood family so acutely that it dragged her down in these days of the relentless march of physical and mental degeneration, we shall never know for no record survives on which we may make an assessment. It seems probable that her niece Polly, at nearby Needingworth, was the only one of her own blood family whom Susanna could visit, or be visited by, on a regular basis.

At Peterborough things were quite different. Just about a couple of years younger than her sister at Sutton, Helen Letitia Duddington was still living at their long–term home, Olive House, with her Carpenter husband, Joseph; they had a few of their eight offspring – some now married – living close by. But time was also taking its toll on Joseph and Helen.

Much the same was true of Charles James and Mary Annie Hercock at Dunstable. And what of their various offspring? Their youngest, Wilfred, still unmarried and living at home with them, had lately joined the Particular Baptist Chapel at West Street, but later was to switch to the Strict Baptists before, eventually, reverting to the Particulars with whom he was to become an accredited Minister, spending most of the rest of his earthly life preaching and ministering for the Cause ... the only one of Henry and Susannah Hercock's grandchildren known to have followed in his grandfather's footsteps. Also still single, Bertram had gone off to the War as a Mechanic in the Royal Flying Corps – but he was to take a short time off from his duties to marry a Dunstable girl, Elizabeth Mary Banks, in 1917. She, sadly, was to die a few years after and, though Bertram was later to remarry (the family's long–standing friend from Potton, Alice Woodman), no children of his own were ever to enter Bertram's life. Annie Christine (known as Chrissie), had married during the summer of 1915 – not many months before her husband, Edwyn Charles Bowen, had enlisted and found himself posted to the Northamptonshire Regiment. Chrissie had then gone to Maldon to live with her eldest sister, Ruth Flowerday, whose husband had also gone off to the War; while Ruth went out teaching to bring in an income, Chrissie minded the two young 'FLOWERDAY' children. But not many months had passed before these two women decided to relocate to Dunstable to be near their parents – hence, they and the two children ended up living in a rented house further along Great Northern Road from the family Bakery. Ruth began attending at the West Street Baptist Chapel where she and Will had been married. Albert, then living in North–London suburbs, had also married during 1915 – at Barnet Register Office, which is unlikely to have pleased his parents much. Edith, 'CJ' and Annie's second daughter, was still unmarried at the time, but no longer living at home with her parents – she'd branched out into the world of work many years earlier when the family had first moved away from Potton; however, she was to marry in Dunstable before long, also in the West Street Baptist Chapel, when she took Albert William Matthews as her husband, in 1917. Finally, Charles Ernest, the 'black sheep', had moved to Croydon (with his wife and children) some time in the run–up to the War (for service in which he had enlisted in 1915). All of 'CJ' and Annie's offspring were to marry in time, and most were to have children of their own.

Although all other of Henry and Susannah Hercock's offspring had now died, there were, of course, living in various parts of the country many more of the couple's grandchildren than those mentioned here. For instance, Eliza Jane Underwood (daughter of Lucy Ann), having married Harry Mumford, they moved first to Eastbourne, Sussex, where she and her husband had begun raising a family, though they'd soon moved to Burton–on–Trent to give birth to their daughter, before moving again – to Hackney in the east of London. Her younger brother, William Henry, had moved from Nottingham with his mother, accompanying her to Derby where he continued to live with her until she moved, finally, to Sheffield. And in Sheffield, Helen Susannah – following her marriage – was living with her husband, Edwin, still in the same house that he had inhabited since before the death of his first wife.

Polly had settled in well at the 'SENESCALL' residence, Rose Villa, in Needingworth's High Street where she was now mistress of a large and busy family home, with servants to do much of the day–to–day work about the house. Her younger brother, Walter, with his wife, Edie, and their three youngsters, were happily ensconced at Romford where not only were they deeply involved in the life of the Trinity Methodist Church, but also in the community at large.

Walter boasted musical talents which led him to play the clarinet in the Romford Town Orchestra. Meanwhile, Walter's younger brother, Fred, and his wife, Flo, had their heads down in bringing up their family, too.

Victor Rex Hurlock

Entirely out of contact with any of these of their cousins, the offspring of Josiah and Lucretia were also going about their lives in the difficult years of the War. Both John Henry and his younger brother, Sydney, had associated themselves with the medical profession: John Henry as an Assistant in a Dispensary, and Sydney as an Assistant to some medical man. The two sons of Josiah's first marriage were completely unknown to their half–siblings by their father's illicit marriage to his second wife. Of those half–siblings, Victor Rex had emigrated to Canada and served during the War with the Canadian Expeditionary Force in Europe; following the ending of hostilities, he settled in Canada where he was to marry and, thus, spawn a new branch of the 'HURLOCK' family in North America.

The most tragic personal loss to the extended 'HERCOCK' family arising from the War was in the death of Eddie Bowen in Flanders during fierce trench warfare and heavy shelling from German positions on Sunday, 13th January 1918. The first his wife, Chrissie, knew of this was in the arrival of a War Office telegram which was delivered to her in Dunstable where she was sharing the Great Northern Road home of her brother–in–law, Will, and sister, Ruth. Ripping open the envelope, distraught, she dashed up the road to her parents – and forever thereafter lived with them, as they were to provide financially for her and her young daughter (who'd been born in 1916, following a period of leave which Eddie had been able to spend with Chrissie). Meanwhile, Eddie's remains had been buried in Cement House Cemetery, Langemark, Langemark–Poelkapelle, West–V., Belgium.

> The grave of Edwyn Charles Bowen, reference XV.D.10, is maintained by the Commonwealth War Graves' Commission whose Internet website has more on him (though it contains some errors of fact).

~ ~

Some time later, Chrissie was to receive a Memorial Scroll of Honour, and a Memorial Plaque which had been cast in bronze, bearing Eddie's name, as a mark of gratitude from the country. This was the outcome of a government–sponsored scheme to ensure that all those who had given their lives in the War were so honoured through these awards to their relations. The Scroll bears the wording: *'He whom this scroll commemorates was numbered among those who, at the call of King and Country, left all that was dear to them, endured hardness, faced danger, and finally passed out of the sight of men by the path of duty and self–sacrifice, giving up their own lives that others might live in freedom. Let those who come after see to it that his name be not forgotten.'*

Eddie Bowen with his wife and infant daughter

The Memorial Plaque, about 5 inches in diameter, came to be known by the crudely undignified title of *'dead man's penny'*. The Plaque awarded in memory of Eddie is nowadays in the possession of his daughter, who keeps it close by her. [Photograph: see page C8]

Britain never really recovered from the First World War – being forever changed for the worse by its harsh and terrible years of suffering and degradation of human values. Just as the older surviving members of the 'HERCOCK' family never got over the losses of their close loved ones through natural wastage occasioned by degeneration of the flesh and intellect. Even though there must have been an acceptance that eventually lives must end, the moment of an ending yet carried with it a numbing shock and stabbing inner pain of irrevocable separation. Next to experience this were Susanna, Helen Letitia and Charles James, when their late dearest sister's husband, William Baxter, reached the end of his life – dying in the depths of winter on 5th January 1920 at Houghton, Huntingdonshire; he was almost 80 years of age. In accordance with his expressed wish, his body was brought, finally, back to his old home to be interred in the same grave as his late wife with whom he was reunited in spirit. The record entered in the Godmanchester **Church Book**, alongside his name where it had been first written in the Membership List some twenty–three years previously, simply states: *'Died at Houghton Jan. 5th 1920·Buried at*

Godmanchester.' [**Godmanchester Strict Baptist Church Book, 1882–1947**: Membership List, page 15] To mark his entrance into the soil and reunification with his Mary, the inscription of the headstone was expanded to its full text which now read:–

> *In Loving Memory of Mary H Baxter, died Jany 24th 1914 Aged 75 years. 'Adoring saints around Him stand, And thrones and powers before Him fall. The God shines gracious through the man, And sheds sweet glories on them all.' Also of William Baxter, died Jany 5th 1920 Aged 79 years. 'Peace, perfect peace.'*

So is marked the last resting place of one of the great Victorian gentlemanly characters, in William Baxter, of the 'HERCOCK' and 'BAXTER' families.

William Baxter was the last of the 'HERCOCK' family group to be interred at Godmanchester. The headstone to Mary Hayes Baxter and William Baxter is now (2011) in poor condition, its surface spalling badly, especially in the middle and lower regions, as the photograph shows.

Mary Hayes and William Baxter's
grave memorial at Godmanchester

The Nonconformist Burial Ground in the Parish Churchyard at Godmanchester was surveyed, and a definitive plan of its grave plots and extant memorials then prepared, by Mr. R. A. Fordham, Architect, in April 1911. In 2001, the Huntingdonshire Family History Society surveyed it again (by which time it had been assigned the 'Block F' reference as a locator in the Churchyard), logging all then extant grave memorials – recording not only their positions on a new ground plan, but also transcribing what they could of the memorial inscriptions.

I have compared these two plans and, additionally using the somewhat muddled old burial records (which had been amended extensively and rewritten several times over the course of the lifetime of the Burial Ground for interments – it was closed in 1959), have correlated all the known 'HERCOCK' family group burial sites between the two plans and annotated my copies of the burial records accordingly. Thus, using the 'FORDHAM' numbering scheme as the main representation below (the Huntingdonshire FHS scheme numbers, preceded by the 'F' reference, are shown in curly brackets for cross–referencing purposes), all the 'HERCOCK' family group graves are as follows:–

No. 361 {F18}: Susannah Hercock (Mrs.), buried 27/03/1907
No. 367 {F22}: Anna Julia Hercock (Miss), buried ?/02/1908
No. 340 {F9}: George Ambrose (Mr.), buried 28/12/1908
No. 341 { – }: Mary Ann Sawyer ('Polly') Ambrose (Mrs.)
    [grave plot reserved, but never used]
No. 430 {F35}: Mary Hayes Baxter (Mrs.), buried 29/01/1914
    [double grave, shared with husband]
No. 342 {F10}: Eliza Jane Hercock (Miss), buried 03/04/1916
No. 430 {F35}: William Baxter (Mr.), buried ?/01/1920
    [double grave, shared with wife]

The graves numbers 340, 341 and 342 are side–by–side, running west to east, indicating reservations of them were originally made simultaneously for intended future use. Of all the foregoing listed graves, it is only No. 361 that is recorded as having a specifically–named Purchaser: 'Miss Hercock' (i.e. Eliza Jane).

+ +

Next of the older generation to fall victim to 'The Grim Reaper' was Helen Letitia Duddington – on 5th May 1921. Her death from Pleurisy, at the age of 74 years, in the home at 14 Walpole Street in the Soke of Peterborough which she and her husband had occupied in marital harmony for such an extended period, whilst in some sense a release into the sweet afterlife for her, must have robbed the ambiance of that family nest of an essential ingredient of its uniqueness and human appeal. For her husband and their offspring, part of the house they knew and loved almost as much as the person died with Helen on that day. It was Helen's daughter Nellie who registered the death, then living at 14 Windmill Street in Peterborough.

Helen, the youngest of the adult female offspring of Henry and Susannah, was buried in the city's large, newer Eastfield Cemetery, on 10th May; and the grave – in unconsecrated ground, signifying her Nonconformist faith – later marked with a heavy, ornamentally carved, granite headstone. Joseph survived his wife by about another eight years; when he finally died, aged 86 years, his body was interred in the same grave in a burial ceremony held on 25th February 1929. Thus are they immortalised on the carved stone:–

In Loving Memory of Helen Letitia the beloved wife of Joseph Duddington who died May 5th 1921, aged 74 years. Also of Joseph Duddington who died Feb. 21st 1929, aged 86 years. 'Blessed are the dead which die in the Lord'

Grave memorial of Helen Letitia and Joseph Duddington

When I first discovered their grave, on 15th August 2002, the heavy headstone was lying flat on its back on the ground. Apart from this, it was in good condition.

A period of about six–and–a–half years passed from the time of Helen's death to the time for her sole remaining sister, Susanna, to go to meet her Maker. She was 83 years old when she breathed her last on 1st November 1927 at her home, North End Villa, in Pound Lane, Sutton, in the Isle of Ely – although not the last survivor, certainly the longest–lived of all the offspring of Henry and Susannah. A niece, Helen Susannah (wife of Henry Markwell), comforted her to the end and registered the death the following day. The ravages of age had been creeping up on the old lady for some time, to the extent that she'd made a Will about twelve months earlier leaving all to two nieces, Helen Susannah Markwell and Agnes Elizabeth Ibbott, both of whom Susanna also appointed as Executrices. When it came to Probate, Susanna's Estate was valued at £30 (something over a very modest £1,200 by today's values). There is no mention of her to be found in the records of the Sutton Baptist Chapel, and no evidence that Susanna Markwell ever transferred her Membership to Sutton from Godmanchester – indeed, in the Godmanchester Membership List the stark entry '*Dead*'

[**Godmanchester Strict Baptist Church Book, 1882–1947**: Membership List, page 15] (without any associated date) written against her name points to her having never severed this particular link with the Chapel and town in which her spirit evidently remained even though her flesh had left it behind on her marriage to William Markwell. Nor is there any evidence of Susanna's burial at Sutton where the small burial ground behind the Chapel building does have some other, earlier, 'MARKWELL' headstones.

> I visited Sutton in 2002 and gave all the visible memorials in the rather neglected burial ground beside the disused, semi–derelict Baptist Chapel building a good looking over, but couldn't find any memorial to either Susanna or her erstwhile husband, William Markwell.

The remote possibility is that she, too, returned to Godmanchester in death, to lie in the same soil as her mother and sisters, but as there is no Monumental Inscription held in the database maintained by the Huntingdonshire Archives, and records relating to the Nonconformist Burial Ground in the Parish Churchyard of St. Mary the Virgin, Godmanchester, do not name her, her final resting place is a mystery. Susanna was, thus, lost forever to her 'HERCOCK' family – both those still living at the time of her departure and those who were to come later. This well–built, confident–looking lady who had had a rather more outward–going nature than many of her sisters and brothers seems to have approached the end of her life in relative obscurity and isolation from any of her 'HERCOCK' relations except, possibly, her niece Polly at nearby Needingworth. So, a doubly sad ending.

◉ ◉ ◉ ◉ ◉ ◉ ◉ ◉ ◉ ◉ ◉ ◉ ◉ ◉ ◉ ◉ ◉ ◉

The Curtain Falls

The last survivor of the original eleven progeny of Henry and Susannah Hercock was, thus, Charles James, himself approaching 80 years of age at the time of his sister, Susanna's, death. He was to live on for about another 18 months beyond this, dying in Dunstable on 10th April 1929. A long–standing Member of the Strict Baptist Chapel in St. Mary's Street, and a well–known personality around the town, his funeral in the Chapel was very well attended, and a particularly moving service which brought together every one of his and Annie's offspring – the only recorded occasion when this happened during all their adulthood years. **The Luton News & Bedfordshire Advertiser** reported thus:–

> FUNERAL OF MR. C. J. HERCOCK.– The funeral took place on Monday of Mr. C. J. Hercock, "Hazeldene," Great Northern–road, who died on the previous Wednesday, in his eighty–first year. Mr. Hercock had been in business as a baker in Dunstable for twenty–two years, and was a well–known figure in the town. He had been a constant attendant and an active worker in the Baptist cause. During his earlier years he was an active temperance worker, and had served as President of the South Beds Temperance Federation. The funeral service was conducted at the old Baptist Church by the Rev. J. Kemp, of Luton, and was attended by many friends of deceased, whose favourite hymn, "Jesus, Thy blood and righteousness,"

1908   1921

Charles James Hercock

was sung. The family mourners included Mrs. Hercock, widow ; Mrs. Flowerday, Mrs. Matthews and Mrs. Bowen, daughters ; Mr. E. Hercock, Mr. B. Hercock, Mr. A. Hercock, and the Rev. W. H. Hercock of Hoxne, sons ; Mrs. B. Hercock, Mrs. W. H. Hercock, and Mrs. E. Hercock, daughters–in–law ; Mr. A. W. Matthews, son–in–law ; Mrs. Senescall, of Needingworth, niece ; Miss Irene Flowerday, grand–daughter. Floral tributes were as follow *[sic]*: In memory of a dearly loved husband, from his loving wife ; In memory of dear father, from Ernie and Edie ; In loving memory of our dear Dad, from Ruth and Chrissie ; In loving memory of the dearest of fathers, from Edie and Bert ; In loving memory of our dear father, from Albert and Lily ; In loving memory of our dear father, from Bert and Alice ; In affectionate remembrance of our dear Dad, from Wilfred and Hilda ; In loving memory of our dear grandpa, from Rene, Laurie, Olive and Beryl ; In memory of a dear friend, from Mr. & Mrs. Aish, Frank, and Daisy ; With much sympathy, from Mr. & Mrs. Hales ; Much sympathy, from Mr. & Mrs. Walter Knight ; With kind thoughts, from Joan and Molly ; In remembrance, from Albert, George, and William (employees).

[**The Luton News & Bedfordshire Advertiser**, Thursday, 18th April 1929: page 6, column 3]

'CJ's interment, on 15th April 1929, was in a grave prepared for him in the Municipal Cemetery of Dunstable's West Street. Here a granite kerb surround, gleaming white in its newness, was duly installed, bearing the inscription:–

In Loving Memory of Charles James Hercock, who entered into rest April 10th 1929, aged 80 years.

It was to be a further twenty–two years before his widow, Mary Annie Hercock, joined him in this grave and the surround had her name added in the words: '*Also Mary Annie, his wife, who entered into rest February 25th 1952, aged 95 years. Re–united.*'

Before reaching the end of his life, 'CJ' had seen all his and Annie's issue marry and, though not all had provided the couple with grandchildren, most had done so by the time of 'CJ's death – so he had had the delight of seeing his family multiply to carry on the 'HERCOCK' name of which he was rightly proud. His closest granddaughter, Rene Flowerday, was even there to see his coffin committed to the grave.

A tremendous mark of her enduring affection and respect for her Uncle Charles James (who had given her shelter during her especially vulnerable teenage years), Polly made the effort to come from Needingworth to bid her last farewell to 'CJ'. For her this was a particularly poignant occasion, for 'CJ's death marked the final fracturing of the last link in the chain back to her own father ... after all, as William Henry's younger brother, 'CJ' had been the sole remaining contemporary of her father to have shared the same blood and to have come from the same gene pool.

For the extended 'HERCOCK' family, the death of Charles James bore an air of singular finality, too, in that he had been the very last living element of the large family of progeny which had been spawned by Henry and Susannah. Moreover, 'CJ's steadfast adherence to the principles by which his parents had lived, his faithful devotion to the Baptist Cause which came from the seed planted in his father some one hundred years earlier, and his loyalty to

Chapel Closures

Even during his lifetime, Henry Hercock bemoaned the declining fortunes of Strict Baptist Chapels and numbers of their Friends.

But in the 20th Century they waned with even greater dispatch, as evinced by the following statistics of closures of some of the Chapels which the Hercocks had patronised in earlier times:–

Yaxley (1913), Cirencester, Park Street (1931), Godmanchester (1959), Leeds, St. James' Street (c.1966), Oakham (1966).

The Godmanchester Chapel building was soon demolished – which would have brought great sadness to the hearts of the Hercocks, as would the loss of Oakham which had been so significantly formative in the early days of Henry Hercock's Baptist faith and life.

his wife and offspring – all these had earned him a notable place in the history of the universe of those millions whose names never go up in lights as great explorers of the unknown, or leaders of nations, yet whose contributions to the book of the world are remarked for the outstanding content of their individual chapters. As his father, Henry, had similarly won himself a place. Yet, despite all this, no obituary to 'CJ' ever appeared in the religious press, echoing the sad lacuna which had marked the demise of his devout sister, Eliza Jane.

And so the closing scene of the earthly performance which this group of the Hercocks played reached its culmination, and the curtain fell at last, silently, leaving the audience of those surviving to wend their melancholy ways from the proscenium of the final bow.

With this, the book of the particular group of the 'HERCOCK' family – that of Henry, of his wife, Susannah, and of their progeny – was closed. Between its covers lies the varied story of a moving sequence of events concerned with lives dedicated to a unique Baptist Cause which flourished in England during the 19th Century, which endured into the 20th Century (though dwindling in strength and influence) and which lingers, enfeebled and often much–transformed, into the 21st Century.

~ ~

Although there is now – in modern times – a significant number of the wider family's graves in Dunstable's West Street Cemetery, the group of 'HERCOCK' family graves at Godmanchester is, perhaps, the most significant of tangible reminders of the manner in which Henry's people lived in support of this Cause. It is a Cause which was the very essence of Henry Hercock himself and which, by dint of his tireless promotion of it, still echoes through the long, branching corridors of the wider family of those descendants from him who live to carry the legacy of his blood onwards to forthcoming generations.

❖ ❖ ❖ ❖ ❖ ❖ ❖ ❖ ❖ ❖ ❖ ❖ ❖ ❖ ❖ ❖ ❖ ❖

Do not stand at my grave and weep:
I am not there. I do not sleep.
I am a thousand winds that blow.
I am the diamond glints on snow.
I am the sunlight on ripened grain.
I am the gentle autumn's rain.
When you awaken in the morning's hush,
I am the swift uplifting rush
Of quiet birds in circled flight.
I am the soft stars that shine at night.
Do not stand at my grave and cry;
I am not there, I did not die.

– Origin Uncertain (English, Anonymous)

❖ ❖ ❖ ❖ ❖ ❖ ❖ ❖ ❖ ❖ ❖ ❖ ❖ ❖ ❖ ❖ ❖ ❖

After Life of the Soul–Mender

PART TWO

Henry Hercock's People : An Assessment

A COHESIVE GROUP

Henry Hercock's People : Summary Appraisal

We cannot, in truth, divorce any consideration of the personalities and lives of Henry's wife (or widow) and their offspring from the assessment of Henry himself and his life (which is embraced in depth in the forerunner to this book, namely **The Shoe–Maker turned Soul–Mender**). However, what kind of a people this small group was has already been demonstrated, in essence. Most of them took their lead from Henry, the principal man in their lives – with the obvious exception that he was the only one who took to the Particular and Strict Baptist faith quite so passionately and utterly.

The lives of a few of this group were sufficiently differentiated for us to know in some depth what the individuals were like and what contributions (whether sectarian or religious) they made not only in the wider family, but also in their local communities. Those who are noteworthy in this respect were Mary Hayes Baxter, Eliza Jane Hercock, William Henry Hercock, Charles James Hercock and Josiah Hercock. Much of what is available and known about these five either is included earlier in this book or has been separately promulgated by me in other works (such as **The Shoe–Maker turned Soul–Mender**).

> See '**Status of this work vis–à–vis previous works**' (in the Introduction) for details of relevant earlier works, and guidance on interpretation in instances of perceived conflict between content of this work and earlier works.

However, insufficient detail has been recorded or discovered, or has survived, of other individual members of this group for us to be able to give with certainty more than the outlines which are included elsewhere in this book ... although Susanna Allen, later Markwell, perhaps falls between the two camps (having been written about, briefly, in an earlier work and more expansively in this work and its forerunner, **The Shoe–Maker turned Soul–Mender**).

What we can say, though, is that as a family assemblage they formed a remarkably cohesive bunch, ample evidence of which has been presented. Whilst the majority of the adult offspring of Henry and Susannah respected their mature and, eventually, ailing widowed mother as Elder of the family, and ensured she received the best possible companionship and care throughout her remaining days after Henry's demise, they also showed tremendous loyalty to each other in the way they lived and spent time with each other, or otherwise remained in as close personal contact as geographical factors allowed; and – above all – in the way they shared a common Particular or Strict Baptist faith and general ethos of family life which their father and mother had given them from the earliest times of their childhoods. It was in their religion and attitudes to life, closely interwoven with their collective blood and genes, that they had founded and retained what proved to be their strongest bond ... a bond which persisted to the very ends of their various lives – and, in many instances, lingered on into relationships between such of their own progeny as survived them. The fact that several of this group chose to live with or near each other in Godmanchester – where they were buried in close proximity to each other – shouts louder than any words could ever do of their individual, enduring commitment to 'family' and the common values which had characterised their lives.

After Life of the Soul–Mender

PART THREE

Appendices

APPENDIX ONE

Who was John Hurlock?

THE ACCOUNT OF HOW I unearthed and disentangled the convoluted life of Josiah Hercock or Hurlock is inextricably linked with my efforts to demonstrate and, ultimately, prove – so far as this is possible in the absence of a sworn statement by the man himself that this is so – that the 'John Hurlock' who emerged in the late 19th Century to marry Nellie Emily Rix, and who subsequently died from the effects of the tragic fire at Harringay in 1905, was actually Josiah Hercock or Hurlock (who had previously married Lucretia Hill and had two boys by her) in another guise. As with solving any mystery, the detective work involved requires at least a modicum of luck if it's to succeed – and, certainly, a generous measure of good fortune came my way in this quest. Without that, I doubt a solution would ever have been found – at least not easily! This story, then, makes worthwhile retelling for its own sake, which is why I've included it here in detail.

When I first heard (from my father and his sister many, many years ago) about the saga of Josiah Hercock, it intrigued me greatly – and I knew that one day I would want to establish the reality of the story. It was not until about 2002 that I was in a position to do that. Then I began by preparing a summary of the known facts and separating them from what was unproven or mere supposition. The known facts (about events independently understood, by several people in different branches of the 'HERCOCK'–descendant family, to have happened) were, briefly, that Josiah Hercock had: (1) taken an alias (of which no details were now known); (2) made a bigamous second marriage (again, no details were now known); (3) suffered in a fire whilst trying to save his wife and children (no further details of the event were now known); (4) died due to the fire (also now known without details); (5) been a Draper; and (6) lived and worked in Leytonstone during the early 20th Century.

It was also known, independently from various 'HERCOCK' folk as well as from official records of Josiah's earlier life, that much earlier information of his true identity, such as his date and place of birth, and the names of his parents, were established beyond doubt.

My father and his sister, and some of their 'HERCOCK' uncles and aunts and cousins, knew only the bare bones of what had happened in the life of Josiah; these rudiments revolved around some of the facts set out above, but also included a certain amount of unproven stuff – hearsay. For instance, my father and his sister knew about Josiah's bigamous second marriage, that he had hidden the reality by assuming an alias, that there had been children by both the first and second marriages, and that there had been a disastrous fire. My father had been given to understand that Josiah himself had died in the fire which had apparently occurred in a shop at Leytonstone where Josiah lived; my father also thought the fire had happened about 1917, though he couldn't say how he came by that year. No–one I spoke to in family circles before 2002 knew much more than this, though. Another family member had, to my knowledge, made efforts before me to find out about the reality of the fire and what actually had happened to Josiah, but without success.

My father had died by the time I made a start on this particular line of 'HERCOCK' research, in 2002, but I did have a candid exchange of information with one of his first cousins, Beryl Croft, to find out what information she had about Josiah, the bigamous marriage, and the fire. She was to provide me with a vital clue. Beryl told me that Josiah's elderly widowed mother, Susannah Hercock, had known about Josiah's having taken an alias and made a bigamous marriage; but that no–one told Susannah about the fire and Josiah's death because they wanted to spare the old lady the pain of hearing that. (Josiah, it was said, had been her favourite son. It appears most other folk in close 'HERCOCK' family circles of the times had also known about Josiah's alias and bigamous marriage – and several had known that he had died in, or as a consequence of, the fire.)

As soon as I had this piece of information about Susannah's having been kept in ignorance of her son's death as a result of the fire, I realised that – of course – Josiah must have died *before* she did; and, knowing

Susannah had died on 24th March 1907, meant that the fire and Josiah's death must have preceded that date. Although it was not then known whether Josiah had died in the 19th or the 20th Century (the latest official information then readily available about his whereabouts and when he was last seen alive came from the 1881 Census), it seemed to me very probable (because of the wider family's success in withholding information about his death from his mother) that he had died in the 20th Century; and this obviously limited quite markedly the range of years when the fire was most likely to have happened ... to 1900–1907. This, I felt, was a very workable range which had never previously been recognised, and could readily be researched.

I had established from the 1881 Census that Josiah had already by then changed his surname from 'HERCOCK' to 'HURLOCK', so that was one more bit of information which was to come in useful in unravelling what subsequently became of him. At that time it was this Census that gave the last–known official sighting of Josiah – living in Whitstable, Kent, with his legitimate first wife, Lucretia, and their two boys. At the outset of my research on him, no death registration for a Josiah Hercock or Hurlock came to light, so I presumed any record of the man's death would have been under his alias name which had yet to be discovered.

On 24th May 2002 I instructed a professional researcher who had previously done some good work for me in searching old newspapers at the Newspaper Library at Colindale, North–London. I deliberately gave her wide terms of reference so as to ensure she would not focus too narrowly on her task, and warned her of the imponderables in the story. I asked her to commence searching at 24th March 1907 (the date of Susannah Hercock's death) and to work backwards in time from that. She got going, and – amazingly – wrote to me on 12th August 2002 enclosing copies of various newspaper reports of a night–time fire in Harringay, London, in June 1905 and naming a 'Mr. John Hurlock', a former Leytonstone resident, who died from burns occasioned whilst trying to save his wife and children from this fire at his Drapery premises. I immediately telephoned the researcher to confirm I thought she had found the right story, even though it was plain that it would be necessary to do more work to prove the identity of this 'John Hurlock'. Soon, she found several other newspaper reports connected with the fire and its consequences – an excellent bit of research which was to result in my satisfactorily solving this great, long–standing 'HERCOCK' family mystery. The full solution was to unfold in stages.

The researcher whose services I used for this work was Rosie Taylor of North–London. Regrettably, Rosie died in November 2010 whilst still working on some other 'HERCOCK' research for me. Her contribution to my 'HERCOCK' research has been very substantial, not least in helping me solve the mystery of what became of Josiah Hercock or Hurlock.

From that beginning I began to collect further information about the family involved in this tragedy, based on newspaper reports and other, official, records which I soon found. Also, I began to make the necessary further investigations to find out whether this 'John Hurlock' was, in fact, Josiah Hercock or Hurlock, although I was already sure in my own mind that he was. The reason I was so sure rested on an old postcard which had come into my possession some considerable time before.

I had seen the postcard several years earlier because it was among a box of photographs and other memorabilia in the possession of my father's sister – she had given me open access to this box and its contents, and I'd copied most of the latter, including the postcard. However, at that time (which was long before 2002) I didn't fully understand the postcard or its significance. It had been posted from Potton, Bedfordshire, in the late afternoon of 1st July 1905, addressed to a *'Mr. Herlock'*, care of a person whose name I didn't recognise, a *'Mrs. Rix'*, at an address (which meant nothing to me) in Essex. The picture on the postcard was of Potton Market Place, and the message written on the other side began: *'Thought you would like to see the old home once again.'* (The rest of the message was trivial.) It was signed *'Love from Ethel'*.

With such an ending, it was obvious to me that 'Ethel' had to be family, from which I knew immediately who Ethel probably was – a daughter of Helen Letitia Duddington, née Hercock, who was one of Josiah Hercock's older sisters (in fact, his nearest–in–age sister, to whom he'd probably been quite close); so Josiah would have been Ethel's uncle. But as this postcard was in my aunt's collection of memorabilia, I was confused as to the true identity of its intended recipient, and at that time thought that somehow it had been sent to my great–grandfather, Charles James Hercock, who, of course, was also uncle to Ethel Duddington – however, the way in which the postcard was addressed did unsettle me, leaving me unsure about it and its meaning.

The relevance of Potton to the story needs to be emphasised at this point. Henry Hercock, Josiah's father, had moved to the town with his wife and a few of their younger offspring early in 1866, as was well known. As Josiah would have been only 13 years old then, it seemed clear he would have been one of those children who moved to Potton. However, I had no official record of his ever having lived in the town: the first Census after 1866, in the spring of 1871, showed he wasn't there then – at this stage of my research that Census, although open to the public, had not been transcribed or digitised so there was no way of using computers to search for folk if their whereabouts were unknown. So it was merely my conjecture, backed up with common sense based on his age, that put Josiah in Potton in 1866 so far as I was concerned.

The postcard, however, clearly had been sent to someone who had lived in Potton – as it's written message, supported by the photograph on the other side, indicated. Again, though, at this time I did think the recipient could have been my great–grandfather, Charles James Hercock, who had lived in Potton from circa 1871 to 1902, running his shop on the Market Place (his former shop featured prominently in the photograph). As he no longer lived there in 1905, the message of the postcard could have fitted him; and, moreover, the fact that the postcard eventually came to end up with my aunt lent support to my idea that it could have been 'CJ' who had been the addressee.

A few years later, long after I'd found out about the reality of the fire, much to my surprise I was given the original of that postcard – I'd forgotten about it in the meantime. As soon as I saw it again, the penny finally dropped! As I then knew that the John Hurlock who'd died from burns received in the fire had previously married Nellie Emily Rix, the way in which the postcard was addressed – 'c/o Mrs. Rix' – suddenly made complete sense! That left me in no doubt that the intended recipient must have been the person I knew, in truth, to have been Josiah Hercock or Hurlock – and the postcard proved he *had* lived in Potton. But, of course, I also now knew that he, in the guise of 'John Hurlock', had died on 3rd July 1905, so could never have received the postcard – had he done so, it could never, I think, have been returned to my side of the family. I assumed '*Mrs. Rix*' probably had been Nellie Emily's mother, acting as a 'post–box' address – another part of the ploy Josiah used to make himself hard to track down had his legitimate wife, Lucretia, or the authorities, tried to do so.

> Much later in my research, I went on to discover that Mrs. Rix was living at 'Oakdene', Meredith Road, Clacton–on–Sea, Essex [From Kelly's Directory of Essex, 1902], but that previously she'd been at 'Thorneycroft', High Street, Clacton–on–Sea, Essex [From Kelly's Directory of Essex, 1894]; no forename was associated with either of these Directory entries, so it is not possible without further delving to identify fully the person concerned.

Another fact that became obvious once the penny had dropped was that the postcard's sender, Ethel, could not have known, when she wrote its message late in the day of 1st July, about the fate which had befallen her uncle Josiah; otherwise she would never have written as she did. She sent the postcard in all innocence, never dreaming how important it was to become all these years later in helping to establish the reality of the deception which her uncle put upon some of the family folk, and others, who held him most close and dear.

It was at that point that I took a break from my 'HERCOCK' research for several years.

⊙ ⊙ ⊙ ⊙ ⊙ ⊙ ⊙ ⊙ ⊙ ⊙ ⊙ ⊙ ⊙ ⊙ ⊙ ⊙ ⊙ ⊙ ⊙

When I returned to it, in 2006, I began the long haul of tracing living descendants of Josiah Hercock or Hurlock, otherwise known – after the 1881 Census – as 'John Hurlock'.

Before long I discovered that John Henry Hercock or Hurlock (first son of Josiah and Lucretia) went on to marry Ada Waddington and, from her, sired three children – first a boy, Raymond, then a girl, Nellie Lucretia, and, finally, another boy, Clifford. John Henry's younger brother, known as 'Sydney', was still unmarried in May 1929 (when his mother Lucretia's Will was Proved to him). I also found out that the three progeny of John Henry and Ada married in their turn and between them raised several children – who were my third cousins. I set about trying to make contact with those whose names and addresses I'd been able to find.

I also found out that most of the offspring of John Hurlock and Nellie Emily, née Rix, who survived the fire went on to adulthood and to marry; though only two of them apparently had

Clifford Hurlock in his prime

offspring. One of these two, having remained in England, had produced only a very limited descendant–line of which a sole male member had died late in 2006, regrettably, before I could make contact with him, though I did manage to make contact with his widow – the first of the 'HURLOCK' folk in the descent–line from Josiah whom I'd succeeded in contacting. All other offspring (and their descendants) from the progeny of John and Nellie Emily Hurlock whom I found still to be alive lived in Canada; this because John and Nellie Emily's son, Victor Rex Hurlock, emigrated there in 1914 and, after fighting with the Canadian Army during the First World War, returned to settle in Canada where he married and raised a substantial family. Eventually, I succeeded in making contact with several of Victor Rex's descendants there. Until I mentioned the fact to them, they had no knowledge of their ancestor John Hurlock's true earlier life (including his earlier marriage) as Josiah Hercock or Hurlock – one of these Canadian cousins had tried researching John Hurlock's earlier life and always drawn a blank (which is no wonder, given that she was working with the wrong name and partly the wrong information about his birth etc., due to his having used the alias to throw people of his trail).

To be absolutely thorough, I have carried out – both myself and with the help of a professional researcher – exhaustive investigations to establish that the John Hurlock who died as a result of the 1905 fire was not someone other than Josiah Hercock or Hurlock. Detailing the significant points of identity of both these men, this is how they both appear, based on what can readily be established (as tabulated on the following pages):–

Josiah Hercock or Hurlock – all the following facts are proven from, or given in, the documents and sources cited

		Information Source(s)----- Supplemental
❖ birth name	Josiah Hercock	birth certificate
❖ birth year	1852	birth certificate
❖ birth date	11th August	birth certificate
❖ birth place	Oakham, Rutland	birth certificate
❖ full initials	J. H.	birth certificate, etc.
❖ father's name	Henry Hercock	birth certificate
❖ father's occupation, 1852	Boot & Shoe Maker	birth certificate
❖ father's occupation, 1855+	Baptist Minister	e.g. Censuses, post-1851
❖ name, 1861	Josiah Hercock	1861 Census ----------- at home, with parents, etc.
❖ birth place, stated 1861	Oakham, Rutlandshire	1861 Census
❖ occupation, stated 1861	Scholar	1861 Census
❖ name, 1871	Josia [sic] Hercock	1871 Census
❖ birth place, stated 1871	Oakham, Rutland	1871 Census
❖ occupation, stated 1871	Draper	1871 Census
❖ marriage date	3rd June 1872	marriage certificate
❖ actual age at marriage date	19 years 9½ months	based on birth and marriage certificates
❖ age stated at marriage	19 years	marriage certificate
❖ birth year implied by age stated at marriage	1853	marriage certificate
❖ name stated at marriage	Josiah Hercock	marriage certificate
❖ marital status (previous) stated at marriage	Bachelor	marriage certificate
❖ occupation stated at marriage	Draper	marriage certificate
❖ spouse	Lucretia, née Hill	marriage certificate
❖ father's name stated at marriage	Henry Hercock	marriage certificate
❖ father's occupation stated at marriage	Baptist Minister	marriage certificate
❖ father's date of death	28th August 1881	Henry Hercock's death certificate
❖ name, 1881	Josiah Hurlock	1881 Census --------- with wife & 2 offspring
❖ birth place, stated 1881	Oakham, Rutland	1881 Census
❖ occupation, stated 1881	Clothier Assistant	1881 Census
❖ spouse, stated 1881	Lucretia Hurlock	1881 Census
❖ offspring, stated 1881	two males	1881 Census
❖ death registration, post-1881 Census	not found as 'Josiah Hercock or Hurlock'	

[continued on next page]

Josiah Hercock or Hurlock [continued]

	Information Source(s)	Supplemental
❖ name & other details, 1891 Census	not found as 'Josiah Hercock or Hurlock'*	
❖ spouse, 1891 ... Lucretia Hurlock	1891 Census	'wife'; husband absent
❖ offspring, 1891 ... two males	1891 Census	living with Lucretia
❖ name & other details, 1901 Census	not found as 'Josiah Hercock or Hurlock'*	
❖ spouse, 1901 ... Lucretia Hurlock	1901 Census	'widow'
❖ offspring, 1901 ... two males	1901 Census	one living with Lucretia
❖ spouse, 1911 ... Lucretia Hurlock	1911 Census	'widow'
❖ offspring, 1911 ... two males	1911 Census	one living with Lucretia
❖ spouse died ... 20th October 1928	Lucretia Hurlock's death certificate –	'widow of Josiah Hurlock'

* or other surname variant spellings

John Hurlock – *the following facts are given in the documents and sources cited*

Information Source(s)----- Supplemental

❖	birth name.....John Hurlock	.....marriage certificate; 1891 & 1901 Censuses
❖	birth year.....1853	.....marriage certificate; 1891 & 1901 Censuses
❖	birth date.....unknown	.....(no birth certificate found)
❖	birth place.....Leicester	.....1891 & 1901 Censuses
❖	full initials.....J. H.	.....marriage certificate, etc.
❖	name & other details, 1861 Census.....not found as 'John Hurlock'*	
❖	name & other details, 1871 Census.....not found as 'John Hurlock'*	
❖	name & other details, 1881 Census.....not found as 'John Hurlock'*	
❖	marriage date.....16th November 1890	.....marriage certificate
❖	actual age at marriage.....unknown	.....(no birth certificate found)
❖	age stated at marriage.....38 years	.....marriage certificate
❖	birth year implied by age stated at marriage.....1852	.....marriage certificate
❖	name stated at marriage.....John Hurlock	.....marriage certificate
❖	marital status (previous) stated at marriage.....Bachelor	.....marriage certificate
❖	occupation stated at marriage.....Draper's Assistant	.....marriage certificate
❖	spouse.....Nellie Emily, née Rix	.....marriage certificate
❖	father's name stated at marriage.....John Henry Hurlock	.....marriage certificate
❖	father's occupation stated at marriage.....Baptist Minister (dead)	.....marriage certificate
❖	father's date of death.....not found as 'John Henry Hurlock'*	
❖	name, 1891.....John Hurlock	.....1891 Census------ with wife & 1 offspring
❖	birth place, stated 1891.....Leicester	.....1891 Census
❖	occupation, stated 1891.....Draper	.....1891 Census
❖	spouse, stated 1891.....Nellie E. Hurlock	.....1891 Census
❖	offspring, stated 1891.....one female	.....1891 Census
❖	name, 1901.....John Hurlock	.....1901 Census------ with wife & 4 offspring
❖	birth place, stated 1901.....Leicester	.....1901 Census
❖	occupation, stated 1901.....Draper Dealer Shopkeeper	.....1901 Census
❖	spouse, stated 1901.....Nellie Hurlock	.....1901 Census
❖	offspring, stated 1901.....two females, two males	.....1901 Census
❖	death registration.....John Hurlock	.....General Register Office Index
❖	date of death.....3rd July 1905	.....death certificate
❖	surviving spouse, 1911.....Nellie Hurlock	.....1911 Census------ 'widow'

[continued on next page]

John Hurlock [continued]

		Information Source(s) ----	Supplemental
❖	surviving offspring, 1911 .... two females, two males	1911 Census ---------	one living with Nellie Emily
❖	surviving spouse died .... 18th February 1961	Nellie Emily Hurlock's death certificate –	
❖	....	--------------------	'widow of John Hurlock'

* or other surname variant spellings

As may be seen from the foregoing, based on all the points of identity that John Hurlock attributed to himself – i.e. not just his name, but also his birth place, marital status, father's name, and so on – I have searched the official records and never been able to establish the merest hint of existence of a person with those details and background prior to the emergence of 'John Hurlock' at his marriage to Nellie Emily Rix. Further, I have also searched forwards from the date of the 1881 Census for a person having the name Josiah Hercock or Hurlock and all the other details of his birth and background that I knew, from pre–1881

Henry Ernest Hurlock
as a young man

days, were true and correct, and have never been able to find such a person – i.e. that person had disappeared from the records. So, when the one suddenly appeared, the

Master Mariner:
the late Peter Hurlock

other suddenly disappeared. All this is about as strong and convincing a case that one can hope to build in support of the other evidence that John Hurlock was not at all who he said he was, but, in fact, Josiah Hercock or Hurlock in another guise.

I have often wondered whether John Hurlock might have confessed his deception to his bigamous wife, Nellie Emily, as he lay on his deathbed. But, though I cannot say categorically, it seems he probably did not. It's clear, from exchanges I've had so far with some of the folk descended from (or related to some such descendant of) John and Nellie Emily, that Nellie Emily did talk to some of her offspring (and other family) about what happened on the night of the fire, for example alleging that John was drunk and that that had a lot to do with why he got so badly burned.

> This information about John Hurlock's allegedly inebriated state comes from the widow of Peter who, sadly, died in December 2006. Peter was a grandson of John and Nellie Emily Hurlock, only son of Henry Ernest.

Given that Nellie Emily was prepared to speak at all about what must have been an extremely emotionally painful episode in her and her children's lives, it would be surprising – in my opinion – for her not to have mentioned at some stage that her husband had been a bigamist with a hidden earlier life, had she known about that. So, as far as I can determine, that is a secret John Hurlock probably persisted in keeping from his illegitimate wife and children. It was, it seems, a secret he probably also kept from his legitimate wife and children who, I presume, he never again saw after he deserted them in the mid–1880s in favour of Nellie Emily Rix. My only reservation on this point rests in the fact that the postcard sent to him by Ethel Duddington was addressed to him via '*Mrs. Rix*': if Ethel knew about his alias and bigamous marriage – sufficient to fall in with his request to send communications to him via this 'post–box' address of his wife's mother – how could it have been that his wife, Nellie Emily, did not know at least something about his wider family? And why would Nellie Emily have accepted that the only possible communications with her husband's wider family could be through the post, sent via her mother?

That details of his deception were known at all to any outsiders comes down to the fact that he did admit it to one or more of his siblings. I think that, in view of the closeness to his sister Helen Letitia, he is more likely to have confided in

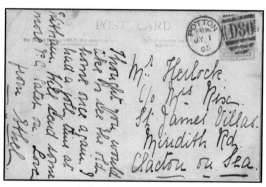

What's in an address ...

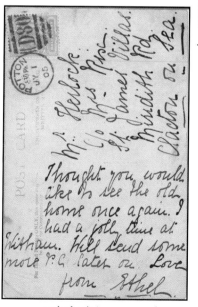

... and what's in a message!

her (and/or her daughter Ethel, with whom we know he had maintained a friendly relationship and exchange) than any other of his siblings. Having said that, I have to wonder about how that vital postcard came to be returned to my side of the family – this in itself might suggest that Mrs. Rix herself sent it to some 'HERCOCK' person whose name and address she knew, knowing that that person was a relation (perhaps, sibling) of her son–in–law; if so, Charles James Hercock would seem to be that person and he, too, would then appear to have been party to the knowledge of what his brother had been up to. This would have provided a route for the story, watered down in detail as time passed, eventually to filter down through descendant generations to reach me from my father.

One last little point worth emphasising, in connection with that postcard, is that which puts beyond all doubt the fact that Josiah had once lived in Potton. Buried in a letter that Josiah's father, Henry Hercock, wrote in 1867 is a cryptic reference to Josiah – written as 'J.' – whose terms make absolutely plain that the lad was then still living at home with his parents. However, it was only during the summer of 2008 that I first noticed and deciphered this reference and, so, was able to say – finally, and without any lingering shadow of doubt – that Josiah had lived in Potton as a youngster. Ultimately, then, the postcard's reference to the fact was validated to my full satisfaction.

❖ ❖ ❖ ❖ ❖ ❖ ❖ ❖ ❖ ❖ ❖ ❖ ❖ ❖ ❖ ❖ ❖

APPENDIX TWO

Sources & Bibliography

THE FOLLOWING IS A LIST of principal sources and other works from which information has been drawn in the preparation of this book. To list all sources in order to embrace the origins of the most minute items of information contained in this work would be pedantic; however, some detailed references to individual sources are made in notes where this is considered helpful or desirable throughout the foregoing main body of the work. The Bibliography refers to works which have provided some subsidiary or background historical information, for which I gratefully acknowledge them.

◉ ◉ ◉ ◉ ◉ ◉ ◉ ◉ ◉ ◉ ◉ ◉ ◉ ◉ ◉ ◉ ◉ ◉ ◉

Principal Sources

NB. Any Item bearing a specific Title has it shown emboldened

Memoir with Last Days & Letters of H. Hercock.
(printed by C. J. Hercock, Market Place, Potton; published by J. Gadsby, London, 1882)

Family Knowledge and Information, including Photographs
(Alan B. W. Flowerday Family History Archive;
and 'HERCOCK' Family Archive, courtesy of various family members –
See Principal Personal Acknowledgements, above)

The Strict Baptist Chapels of England,
Volume 4 : The Industrial Midlands
(by Ralph F. Chambers; published for The Strict Baptist Historical Society, 1963)

Further History of The Gospel Standard Baptists,
Volume 3 : Some Midland and Eastern Churches
(by S. F. Paul, 1958)

The Church Book a record of the proceedings of the Particular Baptist Church
meeting in Salem Chapel, North Street, Peterborough.
otherwise known as The Church Book of Salem Chapel, North Street,
Peterborough (1848–1889)
(held by Peterborough Museum)

The Confession of Faith and Church Covenant, of The Church of Christ;
meeting for worship at Salem Chapel, New Road, Peterborough.
otherwise known as The Church Book of Salem Chapel, Chapel Street,
Peterborough (1865–1926)
(held by Peterborough Museum)

The Church Book Baptist Chapel, Potton
otherwise known as **The Church Book of Potton Baptist Chapel**
(courtesy of Mr. Stan K. Evers, Pastor of Potton Baptist Church)

(The List of Principal Sources is continued on the next page)

Principal Sources *(continued)*

Minute Book
of Potton Baptist Chapel
(courtesy of Mr. Stan K. Evers, Pastor of Potton Baptist Church)

Potton History Society Archives
(courtesy of the Society's Committee, Mr. Peter Ibbett and Mrs. Patricia R. Yates)

Surviving records of selected Particular (or Strict) Baptist Chapels in England
(courtesy of Mr. David J. Woodruff, Librarian of The Strict Baptist Historical Society;
and Miss Marion G. Hyde, Librarian of The Gospel Standard Baptist Library)

Selected Issues of **The Gospel Standard**
(including its 'wrapper' pages)
(courtesy of Mr. Philip J. Neville; and Miss Marion G. Hyde, Librarian of The
Gospel Standard Baptist Library)

Godmanchester Strict Baptist Church Book, 1882–1947
(held by Huntingdonshire Archives, from The Gospel Standard Baptist Library)

Selected Issues of **The Christian's Monthly Record**
(courtesy of Mr. Philip J. Neville)

Selected Sections from an Unpublished Manuscript dating from the 1950s
(by Ralph F. Chambers; courtesy of Mr. David J. Woodruff, Librarian of
The Strict Baptist Historical Society)

Selected Local Newspapers (many held at The Newspaper Library, Colindale, London)
(as specifically named in the main text of this work)

Selected records of Baptisms, Marriages and Burials at the following Parish Churches:–
(NB. This is not an exhaustive list)
Godmanchester, Cambridgeshire (in respect of records of Burials in the
Nonconformist Burial Ground within the curtilage of the Parish Churchyard at
Godmanchester)

Selected records held by the following County Record repositories:–
(NB. This is not an exhaustive list)
Northamptonshire, Leicestershire (including Rutland), Lincolnshire, Bedfordshire,
Huntingdonshire (Cambridgeshire), Nottinghamshire

Records of Burials at Selected Public Cemeteries

General Register Office Indexes of Births, Marriages and Deaths

Selected Birth, Marriage and Death Certificates

Selected British National Census data, 1841 – 1911

Selected Trade Directories

Selected Family Wills

Bibliography

William Tiptaft
Minister of the Gospel, Abingdon, Berkshire
(by J. C. Philpot; published by The Gospel Standard Baptist Trust Limited, 1972 Reprint)

Potton Baptists
The Lord's faithfulness to a faithful people
(by Stan K. Evers; published by Potton Baptist Church, 2005)

The Oxford Companion to British History
(Edited by John Cannon, 2002)

Ancestral Trails
(Mark D. Herber; published by the Society of Genealogists, London, 1997)

Encyclopaedia Britannica

❖ ❖ ❖ ❖ ❖ ❖ ❖ ❖ ❖ ❖ ❖ ❖ ❖ ❖ ❖ ❖ ❖

INDEX

<u>Note</u>: Persons who were relations of Henry Hercock (1811–1881), are indicated in this Index by their relationship to him shown in curly brackets, thus: Hercock, Mary Hayes {daughter}; for convenience and consistency's sake, this applies equally to those born before and after Henry's death.

Persons who were blood relations only of Henry's wife/widow, Susannah Hercock, née Hayes, and not, therefore, blood relations of Henry, are indicated in this Index by their relationship to Susannah shown in square brackets, thus: Hayes, Mary [Susannah's sister].